WE ... OUR BOYS OF COLOR

Part One:
Promising Practices
from the field

Malik Muhammad, Ed.D.
Forward by Damian Watlington

Copyright © 2024 by Abdul-Malik Muhammad

All Rights Reserved

No part of this publication may be reproduced, distributed, or transmitted in any form or by any means, including photocopying, recording, or other electronic or mechanical methods, without the prior written permission of the author, except in the case of brief quotations embodied in critical reviews and certain other noncommercial uses permitted by copyright law. The author of this book has used his best effort in preparing this material. The author makes no representations or warranties with respect to accuracy, applicability, fitness or completeness of the contents of this material. The author shall in no event be held liable for any loss or other damages, including but not limited to special, incidental, consequential, or other damages.

Akoben LLC
364 E. Main Street Suite 1405
Middletown, DE 19709 USA
www.akobenLLC.org

Ordering Information:

Quantity sales. Special discounts are available on quantity purchases by organizations, school districts, and others. For details, contact Akoben at the address above.

ISBN: 978-1-7336862-1-1
Printed in the United States of America

For Sadiki and Damian

Contents

Forward 1
The Invitation 6
Introduction 9

1. The School Experience 18
2. A Complex Problem Needs a
   Comprehensive Solution 41
3. A Special Place for Our Boys: Single
   Gender Environments 57
4. Healing Emotional Pain: Mental
   Health Supports 76
5. Building Relationships And Repairing
   Harm: Restorative Practices 110
6. An Action Plan for Connectedness 142
7. Closing Thoughts 149

Role Models & Resources 152
Bibliography 156
Acknowledgements 161
About the Author 163

Forward

By Damian Watlington

I'm sure that I needed saving, beginning when I was 8 years old, then again when I was 10, 11, 15, and 17. Honestly, this young black boy was in constant need of saving throughout my childhood. The calvary never came for me. Various warriors came through that had an indelible positive mark on my life. Warriors like Sister Francis who gently took my face in her hands and told me that if I didn't learn to love reading, she would tell God on me. There was my 6th grade teacher, Ms. Mamani from Bolivia, who said that I had a beautiful brown face.

There were wonderful friends, more like brothers, like Darin and Raymand, who kept me from losing it to my worst instincts. And in the backdrop, there was always my mom, Rachelann, who endured through all of my thundering years; my dad, Bobby, who exemplified quiet patience; and my brother, Lonnie, who acted like being my big brother was his proudest job in the world. And still I struggled and nearly didn't make it past the negative gravitational pull of abject poverty, family dysfunction, homelessness, racism, the criminal justice system, and my own badass ways.

The calvary never came and the warriors who took care of me did amazing, back-breaking work, but really needed a comprehensive and coordinated plan. They needed to be in community together. I was one of those who was too heavy for a single set of shoulders, I was a community lift.

The picture on the cover is me when I was 17 years old, right in the perfect age to be in the killing fields of American society. It was a critical inflection point for me and even I realized it then. Everything would change. Here is how I got there.

I was born into a womb of trauma. My mom was 6 months pregnant with me when she had to put on the black dress and bury my biological father who had died from a short battle with cancer. I wonder what emotional pain she experienced being with child, taking care of my brother as a toddler, and mourning the loss of her love. I wonder how that emotional pain was communicated to me in the world before this one. I'm sure that right from the beginning, I needed to be saved.

I came forth into a poor family. Unlike some folks, we were poor, and I knew that we were poor. I was born right outside of Washington DC, in Montgomery County, MD, which was then, and still is, one of the wealthiest counties in the U.S. What that meant was that my proximity to wealth and stability was physically close but a million miles away. By the time I was 8, we were homeless, moving between shelters, motels, and living with friends of the family. It was never an adventure, it was unstable, and I needed to be saved.

The first time I got arrested I was 10 years old. I can't remember the details, but I believe that it was for stealing from a store. Over the next four years, I would get arrested at least a dozen more times, spending most of those years in and out of juvenile detention centers and alternative schools. We were living in a Uhaul moving truck at the time because we had been evicted and didn't have anywhere to move our belongings, so we settled into abject mobile poverty. I did things labelled crime partly to get the things we couldn't afford that I wanted and partly because I wanted to rage against a world that I knew was broken and corrupt. I needed the warriors to plan together to come save me from this system and myself.

We started to leave the city on weekends; I realize now that it was to get me away from the streets I was running in DC. We would drive out to rural Pennsylvania, pitch a tent for the weekend, and Lonnie and I would enjoy running around a campground. Immediately after my last day of 8th grade, we left for one of these weekend excursions to Gettysburg PA, except when Monday came around, we didn't leave. My mom explained that she didn't tell me because she knew that I would run away back to DC. She was right. We had moved from the historically nearly all-black city to a historically racist nearly all-white town; and no one was coming to save me.

I was enrolled in 9th grade at Gettysburg Senior High School. It was the 11th school I had attended. We lived in those tents for half of that school year, until it got too cold, and we talked our way into renting a small camper. I'm not talking about a double-wide mobile home, but a small 12' camper designed for a couple to stay over a long weekend. We lived in that camper for the next four years.

My ninth-grade year was difficult due to the culture shock, disconnection from my classmates, and the chip I had on my shoulder for being the outcast, dirt poor black kid. But at the start of 10th grade, something shifted. It was the first time I was in the same school for more than one year which meant that I started developing friendships and could navigate my way around the environment. But most importantly, I met Mr. Terry Fox. Immediately after my first day, first period U.S. History class with him, he surprised me and worked with my guidance counselor to rework all my classes to place me in his honors class. That would literally shift the trajectory of my academic life, as it opened the door for me to take 3 more honors and advanced classes that next semester and throughout the rest of my high school career. Mr. Fox was an amazing teacher, a powerful blend of connection and challenge. With that move on the first day of 10th grade, Mr. Fox would radically help save my mind.

My mom, a working-class white woman from rural Maine, had the clear-sighted understanding that her Black son needed role models who shared the experience of being black and male. She somehow got me connected with students and administrators at the local Gettysburg College. It was at this near-Ivy League, predominantly white private college, that I met Harry Bradshaw Matthews. He was the dean of Intercultural Advancement, but to me, this soft-spoken, glass wearing intellectual, was the epitome of black scholarship. I revered this brilliant thinker who was within my reach. It was he who encouraged me to read the *Autobiography of Malcolm X*. The next day, I stole it from the school library and read it in a weekend. It would change my life. With his example and interest in my commitment to my people, Dean Matthews would help save my spirit.

Over the next few years, I would bump and bruise my way through high school, finding myself eventually with an opportunity and scholarship to Franklin & Marshall College. Lots of things happened while in college, including getting arrested again, leading the first student protest in two decades, and losing my mom to a long, brutal battle with cancer. What shines brightest though is that I would meet the love of my life, Christina. We were married just before our junior year with our daughter, Ngozi, on the way. Most folks around us didn't understand, but that was okay, I was used to being misunderstood. Christina and Ngozi would help save my heart.

I've had a rough journey along the way, but many of us black and brown boys have. Too few of us make it through though. That of course is true for those of us who live close to the killing fields due to poverty. But it is also true for the young brothers who are born with resources but still must navigate the minefields of institutional racism and a society hellbent on taking their bodies, minds, and spirits.

So, I needed the practices outlined in this and the next book. What if I had environments curated specifically for me and other black and brown boys? What if I had access to and engagement with adults who taught me a well-developed emotional vocabulary? What if I was held accountable within a restorative setting instead of a punitive one? I needed these practices as they would have helped save my whole self and made me better for and with others.

This book is personal, not just because Dr. Muhammad writes it with passion for us to save the boys of color in our own lives, or for the sake of his own son, Sadiki, and future grandsons, but because he pulls directly from his own experiences. Not just in serving our black and brown boys who need to be saved, but in being one of those himself.

When I was 14, soon after reading about Malcolm X's life, I closed my eyes, changed my religion, and renamed myself after Malcolm's Islamic name: Malik.

I was born Arnold Damian Watlington and eventually became Dr. Malik Muhammad.

This book is also about me, a boy of color who needed to be saved.

The Invitation

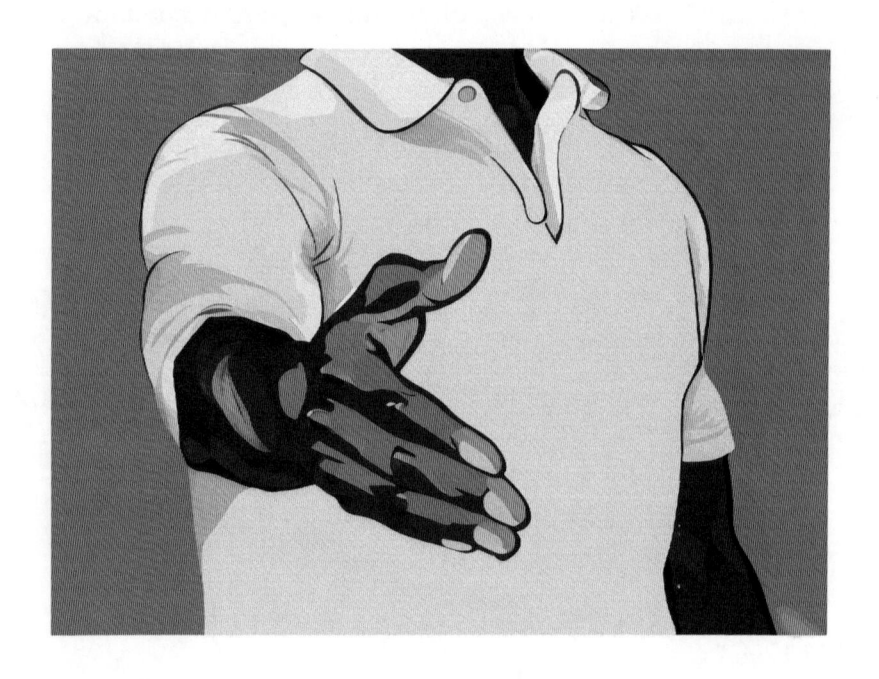

Since 2011, I've been wrestling with, expanding, discussing, and presenting these ideas. This 12-year long process of refinement and sharpening has been arduous. Meanwhile, we have lost too many of our boys along the way. The time is overdue for me to share this work.

I started this project immediately after beginning my doctoral program at the University of Delaware. Like all those pursuing a terminal degree, I was asked to identify an area of study that would weave consistently through my research and coursework in the program. For many, focusing on the finish line is the priority; thus, choosing a narrow scope and manageable project is essential. The path less chosen is a broad-based project that meaningfully contributes to your field. Well, you can already imagine what category the dissertation "We Can Save Our Boys of Color" falls into. It was important to me then, and still is, to leverage the practical and successful interventions done on the small scale, in our schools, programs, and communities, to help save more of our boys. To, at the very least, share those practices far and wide. We have a moral obligation to do so.

In essence, this book is my attempt to fulfill that moral obligation as a scholar-warrior, leader, activist, father, son, and brother.

Throughout the dissertation, I was warned and struggled with scope creep. Scope creep is a real and serious enemy of 'getting it done.' In thinking about this project, which captures the heart of my dissertation and presents it to a broader audience, I've decided to limit the focus here, laying the foundation for the subject and sharing three promising practices. We will explore three additional practices in Part Two and pull the comprehensive plan together.

Let me forewarn the reader that this work is not for the weak of spirit or faint of heart. This book is fundamentally <u>not</u> about improving test scores, academic rigor, or closing the "achievement gap." The change advocated here will also not happen through just recruiting more black and brown teachers/administrators, launching after-school pilot projects with limited grant funds, or appealing to the philanthropic whims of school reform foundations. Truly, this work requires a profound shift in our understanding of, attitude towards, and level of will to address the needs and future of our boys of color far beyond our current level of thinking and service. This is hard work designed for those whose hearts and fighting capacity are built for protracted, committed struggle. If you have found yourself here, remember the following Twi proverb:

> *"One does not abandon their part of the battlefield just because it has thorns."*

This is an invitation to the Struggle together. See you on the battlefield!

Introduction

> **Just when things seemed the same, and the whole scene is lame, I come and reign with the unexplained for the brains 'til things change.**
>
> *Rakim, "The 18th Letter"*

Too many of our Black and Latino boys are dying. Despite the justified outrage at the unjustifiable state-sanctioned murder of our boys in the street by those who should protect them; despite rallying cries of "Black Lives Matter" and mass marches, our Black and Latino boys are dying. They continue to be retained grade levels, dropout, struggle with prosocial coping behaviors, face discipline disproportionality, and interact with an educational system heretofore unable to or unwilling to turn the tide for them. Black and Latino boys score the lowest on every progress indicator. Their rate of suspension and expulsion is exponentially higher, especially compared to the percentage of the population they make up, and they are outnumbered almost 2:1 by their female counterparts in colleges and universities. Many critics have historically and justifiably called public schools in the United States "dropout factories" for furthering the school-to-prison pipeline, especially for boys of color" (Kunjufu, 2010).

The use of the term "save" here is not about paternalism or doing it for them, but rather is the call for us to act with urgency because we are losing them.

This book goes beyond asking *if* there is a connection between the premature and systematic death of our boys of color and the failure of schools to educate them and puts forth a framework of comprehensive and promising practices to disrupt both processes. My essential position is simple: committed activists *must* implement powerful alternative practices within our schools that dramatically lead to saving our boys of color.

I've grappled with the use of the word "save" due to its possible connotations of paternalism and savior syndrome. Am I saying that our black and brown boys are incapable of saving themselves, that they don't hold both the agency and responsibility to change their behavior and conditions to be free and thrive? I'm not saying that at all. The use of the word "save" here is not about paternalism or doing it for them, but rather is the call for us to act with urgency because we are losing our boys of color. Too many of them are drowning in isolation, or fighting for air under the rubble of punishment, or trying to avoid the killing fields of violence and we can do something about it. We can, and must, do everything possible to save them.

This is part of the battlefield that I have found myself working in for nearly 30 years. The discovery of my "heart's work" and purpose was born out of my struggle from homelessness and juvenile delinquency as a boy in Washington, DC, to navigating abject poverty amid a burgeoning and, ultimately, life-altering/lifesaving political and social consciousness in rural Pennsylvania. The confluence of poverty, family instability, community violence, school disconnectedness, and structural racism nearly overtook my life. However, my survival and the subsequent opportunities granted to me by people who loved on me, imbued in me a profound sense of responsibility to serve this population of people. That is, the disconnected, the emotionally wounded, the disenfranchised, yet powerful, strong, and uniquely resilient Black and Latino boys. The question this book asks is:

How can we keep our boys alive and healthy (emotionally, psychologically, socially, spiritually) so that they can mature into men who make a difference, take a stand, are both loving and strong, and have the strength and internal capacity to raise their own families to do the same?

Dr. Malik Muhammad

How I got here

Although a long way from my current role as an organizational leader, I began working on behalf of oppressed communities as a student organizer and leader in high school and college. This focus continued as a teacher and activist in Philadelphia and Baltimore, living amongst and teaching youth in urban middle schools. Here, I began developing educational and social programs specific to the needs of boys of color, including single-gender classrooms and rites of passage programs. After six years of teaching and two in administration, I became disillusioned with the bureaucracy and politics of traditional public education. I left to pursue leadership in adult education, serving marginalized and minority adults as a School Director and Campus President of proprietary schools in Baltimore and Springfield, PA. In these roles, I learned to combine my interest in serving marginalized students with the responsibility to manage resources effectively. At 30, I was the youngest Campus President in the history of the national organization and was given ultimate responsibility over a budget of $6 million. However, after 3 years, I longed for the energy of serving youth and responded to an opportunity to run a failing alternative school in Delaware. In 2008, I became the principal of Parkway Academy in Wilmington, a struggling alternative discipline school serving 180 students in New Castle County, in danger of losing its contract within six months after an abysmal first year.

My departure from the principalship to provide leadership across our system in 2012 corresponded with the launching of four additional alternative programs, housed in traditional public schools. Eventually, we grew these schools and programs to become Delaware's largest alternative education provider. However, I was now the Vice President of Operations for the north region of Pathways, the parent company, and more removed from the good work on the ground than ever. I felt useful but was not working in my passion and on purpose.

Along the way, I founded Akoben LLC, a professional development organization focused on teaching and coaching others how to lead and connect using Restorative Practices, Trauma-Informed Care and Cultural Relevancy & Equity, and Strengths-based approaches. In 2018, I left Pathways to lead Akoben and launch Transforming Lives Inc, a community-based, alternative education organization. As of this writing, Transforming Lives has established 4 alternative schools and 12 alternative programs within traditional public-school settings.

This book shares three of the six promising practices we have learned, developed, and successfully implemented.

The work described in this book pulls through experiences in community-based youth programs, traditional and innovative public, charter, and alternative schools, as well as behavioral health programs, juvenile detention centers, and street-level intervention projects. Through this work, my colleagues and I have witnessed first-hand the failure of interventions for our boys and the success of policies aimed at their demise. Since 2011, we have lost 17 Black or Latino male students to homicide who attended our alternative schools in Wilmington, DE. We refuse to accept these tragedies as normal. However, during the same period, we have helped to save thousands more and learned and implemented several promising and innovative practices along the way. This book shares three of the six promising practices we have learned, developed, and successfully implemented into a comprehensive strategy that specifically addresses the survival of our boys of color.survival of our boys of color.

Dr. Malik Muhammad

But what about the girls?

Since beginning this book, I've had to struggle much more deeply with my own Black male perspective, a singular angle of vision influenced by my experiences with oppression, triumph, and privilege. Ideological challenges raised by my brilliant and fearless wife, Dr. Christina Watlington, and our powerfully deep, conscious daughter, Ngozi Magena, have helped me grow. They continuously and patiently build my consciousness around the struggles of Black and Brown girls and women in schools and beyond. Additionally, I learn regularly from the works of scholar-activists like Dr. Monique Morris, Dr. bell hooks, Dr. Angela Davis, adrienne marie brown, and my close women warriors in Akoben. I stand, unequivocally, with the righteous struggle to make our schools, families and communities sites of life-giving support and liberation for our girls and women. I'm personally drawn to the words of bell hooks when she writes: "This work courageously acknowledges that white supremacist capitalist patriarchy assaults the psyches of Black males and females alike. It is only by constructively articulating the nature of that assault and developing redemptive strategies for resistance and transformation that we can resolve the crisis of Black gender relations." (hooks, 1995) *Our Black and Brown girls are worthy of study, focus, and revolutionary intervention. Our Black and Brown boys are worthy of the same.* I reject the dichotomy, binary, and undeveloped zero-sum analysis that requires us to play oppression Olympics[1]. Instead, we will act and acknowledge that the struggles to

---

[1] Elizabeth "Betita" Martínez, Chicana feminist, in a conversation with Angela Davis on May 12, 1993, responded to a question about coalition building as follows: "There are various forms of working together. A coalition is one, a network is another, an alliance is yet another. ... But the general idea is no competition of hierarchies should prevail. No Oppression Olympics!" (Martinez & Davis, 1994)

support all of our children of color and other marginalized youth are complementary and interconnected. The fight on one part of the battlefield is inextricably linked to the success of another part. For my part, with this book, I'm unapologetically focusing on our boys of color.

A few notes before we begin...

In this book specifically, I'm focusing on Black and Latino boys who are considered biological males or what is described as cisgender[2]. While I don't use the terms biological males or cisgender, I do acknowledge the contemporary discussion occurring around what it means to be male and female. I believe that this conversation can be healthy as we deepen and widen our understanding of masculinity and femininity. For our purposes here, I'm sharing insights and lessons learned from serving our Black and Latino boys who do not identify as transgender or nonbinary. I've had the opportunity to be in dialogue with and learn from several activist educators who focus on serving young people who are transgender and nonbinary. I have a lot more to learn for sure. I believe that we must be committed to understanding and fighting for the humanity of these students. They deserve to be protected and served well. I believe that this work acknowledges and does just that as well for our Black and Latino boys.

This book seeks to accomplish a few primary goals. *First,* I intend to argue that school has not been an overwhelmingly affirming experience for too many of our Black and Latino boys. *Second,* the solution to this challenge must be a comprehensive set of practices that differ from current

---

[2]Cisgender is a term for people whose gender identity matches the sex that they were assigned at birth. For example, someone who identifies as a man and was assigned male at birth is a cisgender man..

approaches. *Third,* provide theoretical and practical field notes for the first three of these alternative practices. *Lastly,* offer guidance on how these practices come together and direction on the next part of this journey in saving our boys of color as I see it.

Along the way, I will consciously:

- Use and legitimize quotes and lyrics from hip hop. Without question, hip hop is, and has been for the past 50 years, the indigenous philosophy for boys of color and many other youth. By calling in the wisdom from this genre, I privilege the voices and speak the language of the marginalized and ignored.

- Flow between using terms like Black, African or African American for boys of African descent; Latin, Latino, or Hispanic for boys of Latin descent; and First Nation, American Indian or Native American for boys of Western Hemispheric indigenous descent.

Chapter Overview

In Chapter One, entitled "The School Experience," we explore how the institution of school, despite being touted as a vehicle for upliftment, has often deepened and amplified negative impacts for Black and Latino boys.

Chapter Two, "A Complex Problem Needs a Comprehensive Solution," breaks down how the common interventions heretofore have failed, been rooted in problematic frameworks, and offers a comprehensive solution for addressing how we can save our boys.

Chapter Three, "A Special Place for Our Boys: Single Gender Environments," introduces the practice of creating spaces specifically designed for our Black and Latino boys.

We will explore how curating spaces for them create the opportunity for them to be understood and thrive.

Chapter Four, "Healing Emotional Pain: Mental Health Supports," addresses the crisis of emotional pain and trauma amongst our boys of color and introduces the practice of gender relevant mental health supports.

Chapter Five, "Building Relationships and Repairing Harm: Restorative Practices," offers a criticism of the punitive approach towards our boys of color and offers restorative practices as a dynamic and powerful way to connect and repair harm.

In Chapter Six, "An Action Plan for Connectedness," we offer practical ways to build up social capital and relationships with our boys of color, which are anchored in and will help enliven the three practices shared in the previous chapters.

Lastly, in chapter Seven, "Closing Thoughts," I bring it all together with understanding the challenges to implementation and the promise of what this work can do for our boys of color and ourselves.

1
The School Experience

> As you recognize the threshold of negative stress
> The crossroads between complete failure and success
> It's so necessary you pay attention in class
> Never tell you the conditions in which to apply the math
> Only sixty-five percent of your peers
> freshmen year, are still here
> And half that total will move on
> But three out of four will drop out in two years
> Add it up and it equals some shit has gone wrong.
>
> *Blue Scholars, "Commencement Day"*

In modern Western society, the idea is sold that education is the greatest and most accessible vehicle for an individual and by extension, his family, to rise out of generational poverty and attain success[3]. The formula is a relatively simple one: strive hard academically to gain access to higher education where you can specialize in a high-value course of study, thus affording you opportunities and choices in career paths and avenues for higher pay and entrance into the middle class. Thus, education is articulated as the gateway and differentiator between job and career, employee and entrepreneur, renter and owner, welfare, and wealth. But what happens when education is not a gateway to success but a trapdoor towards locking one into a cycle of poverty or a prison cell? What happens when your experience with the very institution touted as the answer leaves you disconnected and undervalued? For too many of our Black and Latino boys, this is precisely what the educational system represents.[4]

We have heard and used terms like "crisis" and "epidemic" when referring to the life experiences of boys of color. Additionally, over the past two decades, "achievement gap" and "school-to-prison pipeline" have become popular, characterizing the continued dire state of the educational life of our boys. Indeed, by every positive educational and social indicator, boys of color are experiencing not only comparative, but in most cases, absolute lack of success.

---

[3] Let us not explore here the understanding of education in any society as the transmission of culture. In this very accurate perspective, the educational system (in any form) is primarily designed to transmit the ideology and values of the dominant society. Thus, in the capitalist society, school will imbue values of individualism, competition, and dichotomy. For more read Education and Capitalism by Sarah Knopp and Jeff Bale.

[4] Thus, according to the perspective above, the system is successful in achieving its purpose after all.

Quick Stats on Black & Brown Boys

36% of all Black and Latino boys live in poverty. This is more than double the poverty rate for White and Asian students

Kids Count Data Center, Children in Poverty 2014

40% of students expelled from school are Black and Latino boys, although they only make up 21.7% of all students

Civil Rights Data Collection, US DOE, 2017-18

4x higher dropout rate for Black and Latino boys than white male students. It is even higher for Latino males not born in the US

National Center for Education Statistics, 2016

56% of all school-related arrests are for Black and Latino boys

Civil Rights Data Collection, US DOE, 2017-18

We Can Save Our Boys of Color

The data is indisputable and unavoidable. I've chosen to not dwell here on presenting data, as every school district we have worked with has access to its disaggregated data on academic achievement, graduation rates, discipline and other performance indicators by race and gender. And in every one of those districts there is a similar picture of what is going on with our boys of color. Here are a few statistics that illustrate the situation nationally[5]:

Schools significantly contribute to negative life trajectories for our boys of color through both disproportionate disciplinary practices and inadequate academic service. According to the Task Force on the Education of Maryland's African American Males, a group comprised of college presidents and superintendents working alongside inner-city volunteers and advocates, "there [has] been a fundamental failure on behalf of our African American male students and a persistent bias against them" (Task Force on the Education of Maryland's African American Males, 2006). Several school practices that support these negative educational trends for boys of color include:

- school beliefs that primarily blame boys of color and their parents for poor educational performance (Lynn, Bacon, Totten, Bridges, & Jennings, 2010),

- fallacious and culturally biased teacher/administrator perceptions of their behavior (Thomas, Coard, Stevenson, Bentley, & Zamel, 2009)

- the absence of culturally relevant teaching styles for boys of color (McDougal, 2009)

---

[5]These and more statistics found at Kids Count Data Center, Children in Poverty (https://datacenter.aecf.org/), National Center for Education Statistics (https://nces.ed.gov/), and Civil Rights Data Collection (https://ocrdata.ed.gov/)

- significant racial/gender mismatch and the lack of staffing diversity to support boys of color (McGrady & Reynolds, 2012)

This blend of negative school practices most significantly affects how Black and Latino boys interact with the discipline process. The research clearly shows that school-based practices and their confluence with the judicial and legal system ominously impact boys of color. This relationship was described by Wald and Losen (2003):

A related educational trend that is proving to be particularly problematic for minority students involves school discipline. Since the early 1990's, many school districts have replaced a system of graduated sanctions with a "zero tolerance" approach to wrongdoing.... Minorities are heavily overrepresented among those most harshly sanctioned in schools.... In recent years, several new terms have gained currency in public discourse to describe the cumulative impact of these inequalities and policy shifts: "the prison track," and the "school-to-prison pipeline." These phrases refer to a journey through school that is increasingly punitive and isolating for its travelers—many of whom will be placed in restrictive special education programs, repeatedly suspended, held back in grade, and banished to alternative, "outplacements" before finally dropping or getting "pushed out" of school altogether. (Wald & Losen, 2003)

In case more research evidence is needed, here is a visual:

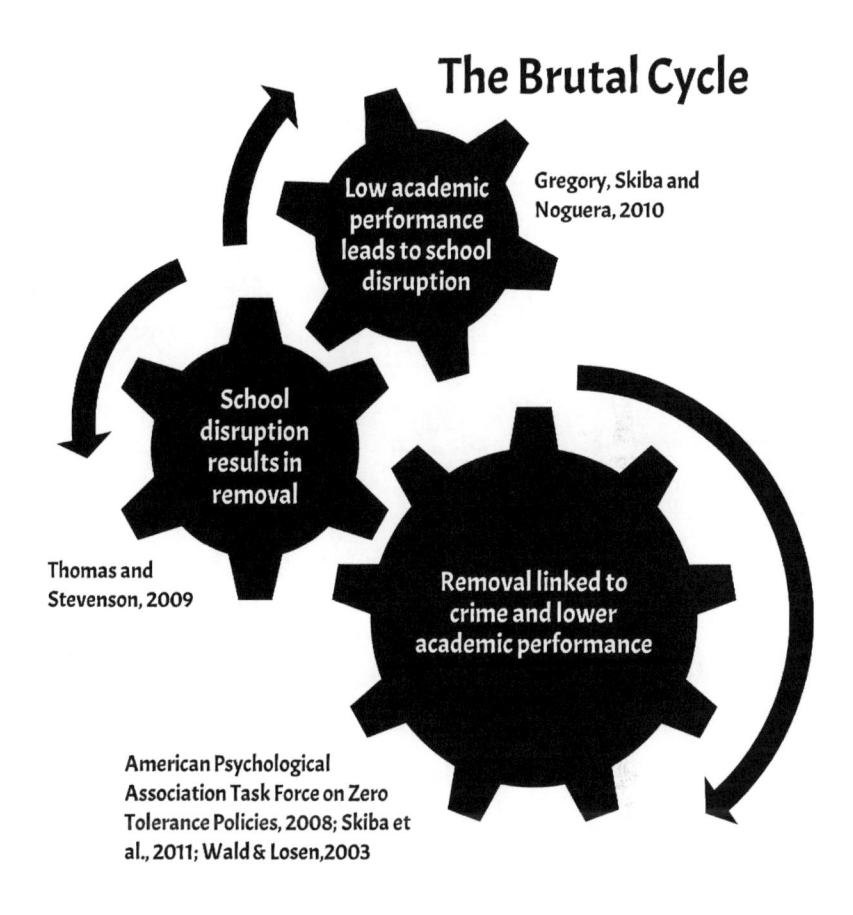

The Brutal Cycle

- Low academic performance leads to school disruption — Gregory, Skiba and Noguera, 2010
- School disruption results in removal — Thomas and Stevenson, 2009
- Removal linked to crime and lower academic performance — American Psychological Association Task Force on Zero Tolerance Policies, 2008; Skiba et al., 2011; Wald & Losen, 2003

In 2010, the College Board published a report based on two years of quantitative data to understand the outcomes of the current educational challenges facing boys of color (Lee, 2010). They identified six (6) possible postsecondary pathways for 15-24 year-old boys of color, including: postsecondary education, military, employment, unemployment, incarceration, and death. Based on their findings, Black males are 50 times more likely to be incarcerated and three times more likely to die by age 24 when compared to white females. In fact, by age 24, nearly 52% of Black and Latino males will be unemployed, incarcerated, or dead. This 2008 data did not even include the nearly 12% Black and 22% Latino male dropouts whose pathways might look bleaker than those with diplomas.

Dubois' Unanswered Question

From a psychological and emotional health perspective, what do these experiences with school mean for our boys of color? *Can we imagine that ten-year-old Samuel could remain unscathed after engaging in an educational process touted as salvation, but he finds none there?* In the face of a personal history of disconnection, bias, harsher punishment than his classmates and oft-repeated statistics that show this common story for those who are like him, he is told that these failures are his own fault. In his 1903 brilliant work <u>The Souls of Black Folk</u>, WEB Dubois asked the most poignant of questions, still relevant to the context of Black and Latino boys over 120 years later:

> *"Between me and the other world there is ever an unasked question: unasked by some through feelings of delicacy; by others through the difficulty of rightly framing it. All, nevertheless, flutter round it, instead of [asking] directly, how does it feel to be a problem?"*[6]

---

[6]This book is a must for any serious student of struggle and liberation ideology: Du Bois, W. E. B. The souls of black folk; essays and sketches. Chicago, A. G. McClurg, 1903. New York

For our boys of color, *how does it feel to be a problem* for schools and what effect does their current experiences have on their lives, above and beyond the school to prison pipeline? To answer this question, we can borrow heavily from Dr. Victor Rios' work in Punished.[7] Rios explores several deleterious outcomes of the punishment paradigm our Black and Latino boys face, including negative credentialing, the youth control complex, and labeling (stigmatization). To this, I add trauma-inducing practices and learned helplessness. Let's break each of these down:

Negative Credentialing

What does every suspension, write-up or retained grade represent within the context of schools? We can think of them as a *negative credential,* a persistent classification or label which determines access or denial to future opportunities. How many suspensions, phone calls home for discipline or disciplinary referrals do we need before we have created a powerfully negative record justifying the removal and placement in an alternative setting or arrest of our boys of color? How many years would a student remain in ninth grade status before opting to formally quit school? **As we review the academic and discipline portfolios of our boys of color, the negative credentials accrued (or assigned) often outweigh the positive credentials--honor roll awards, gifted and talented designation, and perfect attendance certificates.** According to Rios, "negative credentials [also] come in the form of the criminalization of style and behaviors labeled as deviant at school, by police, and in the community. Institutions in the community coalesce to mark young people

---

[7]Dr. Rios is a brilliant thinker and his work has been instrumental in my own journey. Definitely check out Rios, Victor M. (2011). Punished : policing the lives of Black and Latino boys. New York :New York University Press.

as dangerous risks for noncriminal deviant behavior and, as such, deny them affirmation and dignified treatment for stigmatizing and exclusionary practices. (Rios, 2011)"

For too many of our Black and Latino boys, schools have become environments where they gain experience and practice in disconnecting. Here, we can make note of the "10,000 Hour Rule" derived from the work of Anders Ericsson, but made popular by Malcolm Gladwell in *Outliers*. Simply put, the 'magical' amount of time needed to develop expertise in a musical instrument, sport, or other skill is around 10,000 hours.[8] For the young musical protégé to attain critical acclaim by age 20 or for the standout AAU basketball player to get drafted into the NBA after his sophomore year at college, it would require roughly 3 hours of dedicated practice per day over ten years under the direction of a skilled professional. What does all this have to do with the school experience for our boys of color? Seventh grade. **By seventh grade, our boys of color have experienced just over 10,000 hours of school. This includes 7 hours per day of practice (often facing bias in discipline and academic instruction as well as earning negative credentials), for 180 school days per year since kindergarten under the direction of skilled professionals.** By seventh grade, which is when we see many of our boys facing their greatest disciplinary challenges, too many of our boys and their schools have developed an expertise in disconnection, disengagement, and failure vis-à-vis each other.

---

[8]It must be noted that the 10,000 hour rule has been criticized as being over-simplistic. However, even its critics acknowledge the determining role of hard work and dedicated practice. While this does not guarantee expertise, as we must consider other factors like raw talent and access to skilled coaches and mentors, it does provide a benchmark to understand the effects of sustained engagement.

If we consider the number of hours some of our boys face in unstable home environments, challenging family units and structural violence and poverty outside of school, many have accumulated their 10,000 hours much earlier than seventh grade.

Youth Control Complex

Rios describes a 'web of institutions'—schools, families, businesses, residents, media, community centers, and the criminal justice system— that collectively punish, stigmatize, monitor, and criminalize young people in an attempt to control them (pg. 40)." He aptly calls this the **Youth Control Complex.** In essence, the very structures, whether formal, informal, or indigenous, in place to build and support our young men are operating under the unifying belief that to do so effectively, requires these boys to be controlled, dominated, and kept in line. **Their music, dress, play, language, disconnection to traditional faith centers, and styles of interaction are condemned and viewed through an adult gaze that misinterprets expression as aggression, dangerous, and needing to be tamped down.**

How long does it take?

7	hours per day, often with bias and discipline disproportionality
x 180	days in a traditional school year
x 8	years of negative credentialing since kindergarten
10,080	hours for expertise in disconnection and disengagement

Many of our boys reach this negative milestone by the end of their seventh school year

The Youth Control Complex operates within the paradigm of "High Challenge/Low Connection" or "TO" mentality (a more in-depth analysis will be provided in Chapter 5). When schools make students walk through metal detectors, it exemplifies control and doing something TO (search) the young man. When community centers suspend, it exemplifies control and doing something TO (isolate) the young man. When random adults call one a thug, it signifies control and doing something TO (label) the young man. Taken together and accounting for frequency, these acts cease to be individual indignities but rather a "unique formation... taking a toll on the mind and future outcomes of this young person (Rios, pg. 40)."

Possibly the most tragic of all is that even well-intentioned men of color, us old heads who've faced down our own years of the Youth Control Complex, often perpetrate it with hyper-masculinity in the form of fear, intimidation, and alpha male posturing [see "Look at Me Boy" caption]. **Too often, the men who should, must, and do understand our boys best unwittingly become part of the machinery to control and alienate them. This is the deeply uncomfortable to hear, but necessarily vulnerable, truth-telling needed when I, and my adult brothers, look in the mirror and at each other.** Let me be clear, these actions, often rooted in positive intentions, are not the primary cause of the challenges facing our boys and are most frequently acted out by men with little institutional and structural power.

"Look At Me Boy"

"Let's get one thing straight from jump, you do not need to try to be hard here...I'm the Alpha Male and you are in my house now!" That was the first thing that I would say to many of my young male students as a classroom teacher and later as a principal. The message was delivered while I was still firmly shaking their hand and placed another hand on their shoulder for emphasis and a display of dominance. That was only one such signal of power and control. Using my physical presence, violating personal space and "gritting" at boys were all consciously or unconsciously designed to intimidate, invoke fear, and wield masculinity. Years of practice and street culture had convinced me that those were the proven paths to respect and control.

Dr. Malik Muhammad

I believed that I was filling a void for my boys; that I was both modeling for them what a strong man looked like and providing them with the opportunity to engage with an authority that would hold them accountable and in check.

A powerful personal lesson was given when I first met Dashawn, a reportedly aggressive but scrawny 12-year-old Black boy who had been sent to my school for hitting a female student. When we first met, I placed myself squarely in front of him so that he could feel the physical difference, leaned in uncomfortably close, put the full bass in my voice and quietly asked him if he thought it would be okay to get hit like that. When he held his head down and didn't respond, I placed my hand on his shoulder and said, "look at me boy." Dashawn slowly raised his head and I noticed that both of his eyes were welled up with tears and there was a slight tremble in his lips. He was terrified. I was teaching him not to be aggressive by being aggressive.

I mistakenly believed that what Dashawn (and many of my other boys of color) needed was dominance, control, and authority. However, what I realized at that moment, and have been learning ever since, is that they also need warmth, support, and loving-kindness from adult men as well. I reached down and gave Dashawn a hug that first day and began to realize that my boys deserved a powerful, loving leader, not just an alpha male.

Labeling and Shame

What happens when we create environments where our boys feel disconnected, targeted, and experience repeated failure in performance under cultures of compliance vs. connection? Our boys certainly begin getting labeled as troubled, troublemakers, hard heads, high-flyers, problems, challenging students, at-risk, deviant, or thugs. This labeling process is profoundly linked to shaming. According to Johnathan Braithwaite[9] "much effort is directed at labeling deviance, while little attention is paid to de-labeling, to signifying forgiveness and reintegration, to ensuring that the deviance label is applied to the behavior rather than the person, and that this is done under the assumption that the disapproved behavior is transient, performed by an essentially good person (Braithwaite, 1989)." The labels, often perpetual and lasting across institutional contexts, directly lead to stigmatization, or what Braithwaite calls "disintegrative shaming." Rios argues that our boys suffer from the "criminalization of style and behaviors labeled as deviant at school, by police, and in the community (pg. 39)." In other words, **core aspects of their very nature and culture are seen as incompatible with institutional [excluding prison] culture.** Rios goes on to say, "institutions in the community coalesce to mark young people as dangerous risks for noncriminal deviant behavior and, as such, deny them affirmation and dignified treatment through stigmatizing and exclusionary practices. As a result, young people strive for dignity, so that their social relations, interactions, and everyday activities become organized around maintaining their freedom and feeling empowered in a social landscape

---

[9] I'm a big fan of how Dr. John Braithwaite, an Australian criminologist, contrasts stigmatizing shame to reintegrative shame and connects them to social control. Check out J. Braithwaite, *Crime, Shame and Reintegration*, Cambridge: Cambridge University Press, 1989.

Dr. Malik Muhammad

that seems to deny them basic human acknowledgment (Rios, 2011)."

In the face of these sites of disintegrative shame and stigmatization, many of our boys seek to meet the very human and universal need for belonging and empowerment by bonding together in their outcast status and often in their unifying street identity. A respected scholar and close friend, Dr. Yasser Payne, is a leading voice in the study and research around the role of the "streets" as a site of resiliency for Black men and boys. He asserts that "as a strategy for coping with these [school] conditions, these boys may organize their identities around aspects of their lives related to street life—a space where they are seen and see themselves as competent, productive, and resilient. Unfortunately, schools do not provide such a space for street-oriented boys (Payne, Starks, & Gibson, 2009)." My experience is that this often holds true for non-street-oriented Black and Latino boys as well.

> **As a result, young people strive for dignity, so that their social relations, interactions, and everyday activities become organized around maintaining their freedom and feeling empowered in a social landscape that seems to deny them basic human acknowledgment.**
>
> *- Dr. Victor Rios*

Not surprisingly, since school is often a site of negative shaming and stigmatization through labeling, it further alienates many boys of color from the very social embeddedness that would improve their school behavior and performance. We can hear very clear logic in the following statement from Oscar, a Latino male former student sent to our alternative school:

"Look, Dr. Muhammad, my school doesn't like me, and I don't like it. If they are going to mess with me every time I go there by suspending me because of the way that I dress or for other dumb stuff, then I'm not gonna go or I'm going to go and act up so that I don't have to be there. They don't care about me man. They tell me that I need that paper [diploma] but I gotta find another way."

In Chapter Five we will revisit the topic of shaming and how it can be used restoratively and appropriately to build social cohesion, reintegrate, and transform behavior among our boys of color and the adults who serve them.

Trauma Inducing Practices

If we accept that too many of our boys of color face adverse life conditions outside of school—including community violence, structural racism, police bias and brutality, family instability, and poverty—then we must accept that many live with trauma. My wife, colleague, and thought partner, Dr. Christina Watlington, a clinical psychologist, and expert on trauma, explains that trauma is the overwhelming of one's ability to cope.

The Adverse Childhood Experiences Study (ACEs) Questionnaire identifies ten categories of traumatic experiences (1 – 10). In his Philadelphia ACE study, Dr. Roy Wade applied the ACEs to an urban population, adding five new definitions of trauma to the original ten (11 – 15). These expanded categories, now more inclusive of the lived experiences for many boys of color, include:

1. Physical abuse
2. Sexual abuse
3. Verbal abuse
4. Physical neglect
5. Emotional neglect

6. Having a family member with depression or diagnosed with a mental illness.
7. Having a family member with alcohol or substance addictions
8. Having a family member in prison
9. Witnessing a mother being abused
10. Losing a parent to separation, divorce, or other reason
11. **Experiencing racism**
12. **Witnessing violence**
13. **Living in an unsafe neighborhood**
14. **Being placed in foster care**
15. **Experiencing bullying**

We can imagine how traumatic experiences can interrupt or challenge even an optimal, high-functioning learning environment. What happens when the learning environment itself is also dysfunctional? Science tells us that a negative learning environment impacts four components of mental health: learning, externalizing problems (e.g., fights), interpersonal behavior (e.g., forming friendships), and internalizing problems (e.g., anxiety and sadness). When the school environment includes labeling, negative credentialing, stigmatization, control, and a punitive paradigm, it can literally induce and perpetuate trauma and exacerbate its symptoms. The brain of the child [and adult] facing trauma primarily focuses on survival. **For some of our boys, survival manifests as false bravado and hypermasculinity for security, defiance, and opposition to gain control, or disengagement/dropping out and numbing (drugs/alcohol) to remove the threat mentally and emotionally.** As Dr. Watlington

> **❝ Survival trumps learning every time.**
> *Dr. Christina Watlington*

explains so poignantly: "Survival trumps learning every time." We often expect our boys of color to think critically about history, science, math, and English, but create conditions that activate the fight, flight, or freeze response.

Ta-Nehisi Coates describes a dialectical relationship between the trauma of the streets and trauma in school in his book *Between the World and Me* [we see that his title comes from the earlier quoted Dubois' statement]. He writes, "if the streets shackled my right leg, the schools shackled my left. Fail to comprehend the streets and you gave up your body now. But fail to comprehend the schools and you gave up your body later (Coates, 2015)." What Coates is describing here is when the streets are not the kind of site of resiliency and positive power as described by Dr. Payne. Coates continues:

> "I came to see the streets and the schools as arms of the same beast. One enjoyed the official power of the state while the other enjoyed its implicit sanction. But fear and violence were the weaponry of both. Fail in the streets and the crews would catch you slipping and take your body. Fail in the schools and you would be suspended and sent back to those same streets, where they would take your body."

Lastly, according to Dr. Watlington, numbing with drugs, alcohol, sex, and denial is what primarily maintains anxiety and trauma. In my experience, many of our boys experiencing trauma cope in this way.

Learned Helplessness

What happens when our boys face repeated negative credentialing, stigmatizing labels, a youth control complex, and trauma-inducing environments? Our Black and Latino boys are confronted with actual negative conditions that are largely out of their control, yet they are fed a steady diet of lectures that they are responsible for their own lives. **What happens when you are told that you *should* be powerful, but don't have power?** According to Eric Jensen in *How Poverty Affects Classroom Engagement*, "many kids feel like the world "happens" to them. In psychology, this mindset is referred to as a low locus of control. When a person is confronted with an adverse situation and feels limited control to manage it, his or her brain feels stress. The more stress children experience, the more they perceive events as uncontrollable and unpredictable—and the less hope they feel about making changes in their lives (Jensen, 2013)."

This process is called "learned helplessness" because one has learned to become helpless, to accept their station because they perceive their conditions to be inescapable and out of control. There is some linkage between learned helplessness and clinical depression and mental illness.

I provided the following example for colleagues at a recent conference:

Imagine that you are facing a huge bear in the wild. You can't remember which response is appropriate for a grizzly or black bear, especially given that your pre-frontal cortex has given way to your limbic system and reptilian brain since you are now in survival mode. You realize you have three choices: run (flight), put your arms up and appear bigger (fight) or lie down in a fetal position (freeze). *Most* of us would agree that sitting down and engaging with the bear in a "respectful" interaction isn't a serious option. Comparatively, when facing a system that has failed them and continues to negate their humanity at times, our boys of color must make similar choices. They will run (dropout/flight), put their arms up and appear bigger (defiance/fight), or lie down in a fetal position (learned helplessness/freeze). **Why is it that only *some of us* would agree that sitting down and engaging with that system in a "respectful" interaction isn't a serious option.**

Two doomed choices

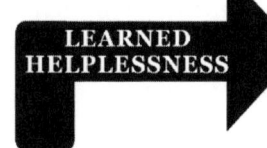

LEARNED HELPLESSNESS →

Micah begins to fail to respond to questions or requests, displays passivity, slumped posture, and disconnects from peers or academics.

Micah returns to English class after 3 days of out-of-school-suspension. He is immediately given a test on material that was covered while he was absent. When he protest, he is told that it was his and his parent's responsibility to pick up the work during his absence.

Both choices increase stress and lead to more disengagement

Micah attempts to strengthen his locus of control by becoming loud, showing aggression and cursing the teacher out, thereby getting suspended again.

REACTIONARY →

In this example, Micah is damned if he does and damned if he doesn't. The well-worn pathway, which is often encouraged by adults who care for him, often leads to the learned helplessness which leaves him in school (at least for now) but left without agency and power.

Images courtesy of Lynlen Mabala

Dr. Malik Muhammad

For our Black and Latino boys, we tend to focus only on the problems with two of those choices, dropping out and defiance. We fail even to recognize the problem with their learned helplessness. Once we overlay notions of masculinity, SES, and normal adolescent yearning for control and self-power into this process, we begin to see how promoting/believing external determinism negatively impacts our boys' emotional and educational lives.

By and large, schools have failed in their stated purpose to educate and transform the lives of our boys of color or have succeeded in maintaining the status quo-- dominant social relationships based upon hierarchies of race and gender in a capitalist society.

However, to leave it there would be a gross overgeneralization and misrepresentation of our boys and the schools that serve them. I have had the honor to work alongside and learn from outstanding educators and activists who have committed their lives to serving marginalized youth, specifically boys of color. From a San Diego public school that is committed to Restorative Practices, to a Humanist school in Maine, from organizations like the Coalition of Schools Educating Boys of Color (COSEBOC) to the powerful former Prestige Academy in Delaware, these institutions and the warriors who work within them have refused to retreat from the battlefield. They are the "Ankobia," *(a Twi term that refers to those who lead in battle),* setting the standard for courage and commitment.

Yet, despite our efforts, we continue to lose too many of our boys mentally, emotionally, and physically. We need more people in this work (in the boat together), using proven strategies (rowing in harmony) to save our boys (in the right direction). In the next chapter we will explore why we still keep losing our boys and introduce a blueprint for launching or deepening the impact of this work.

Reflection & Application

1 **Look at your own data:**

Take a moment now to look up the data in your district on how Black and Latino boys are doing. Look first at the district's website, then the state, and finally at https://ocrdata.ed.gov/.

- Are you easily able to find the data by race and gender?
- Does the data mirror the national statistics?
- What other data points might you consider?

2 Look at the four bullet points on pg. 31. Which of these is most prevalent in your school or the schools in your area?

3 Imagine being asked the powerful question from Dubois: How does it feel to be a problem? Take a moment to jot down some feelings that come up for you with this question:

_____

_____

_____

_____

_____

_____

4. Reflect back on the story in the caption entitled "Look at me boy." What beliefs and assumptions was I making about myself and our boys?

About myself	About our boys

5. Look at the expanded list of Adverse Childhood Experiences (ACES). Did you experience any of these traumatic events yourself? If so, how does this inform and influence your work with and for our boys of color?

_____
_____
_____
_____
_____
_____
_____
_____
_____

2

A Complex Problem Needs a Comprehensive Solution

> Our linear vision is too distorted
> We think in terms of A, then B, then C, then D, then so on. We say "this began here, that ended there"
> So our conversations can have something to grow on.
>
> KRS-One, "Meta-Historical"

In the previous chapter, we established the dire crisis facing black and Latino boys in the United States and the complexities of that problem. But where do we go from here? What are the critical next steps for those of us most concerned with addressing the challenges and current trajectory for our boys of color? How do we disrupt or interrupt this current path?

Let us first start with a clear delineation and identification of what doesn't work. Interestingly, these approaches, disguised or clothed as support programs and interventions, are precisely the causes of our present outcomes. Many current strategies to serve and address the concerns of our boys of color are rooted in one of these four approaches.

Cultural Imperialism

Let's take an uncomfortable look at what the tactics of imperialist colonialism can teach us about current practices with our black and Latino boys. Within the historical and geopolitical context, the process of colonialism involves at least two strategically similar, but tactically different approaches: assimilation and subordination. The colonialism employed by the French and English throughout the world highlight these differences in tactics.

In general, French colonialism was rooted in assimilation. That is, to be recognized, heard, or seen, one would need to adopt the traditional mannerisms, values, and worldview of the Frenchman. Colonies were considered Francophone, and its people were made to understand that to achieve success, or at least eke out a standard of living just above survival, they would be required to forego their traditional values, relationships, and cultural norms in place of their oppressor's. What we see promoted in several contemporary, 'research-based' strategies to serve our boys of color is the advocacy of assimilation. Hierarchical distinctions are drawn between the values and mindset of the poor, middle class, and wealthy, always to the detriment of the poor where many of our black and Latino boys find themselves. Teachers and administrators are trained to identify their own cultural norms, rather than challenge and deconstruct them. Then, they attempt to superimpose those norms inside of our boys of color. Therefore, we dehumanize our black and Latino boys with this approach, often communicating that their values are "less than" and incongruent with achievement, high-performance and success. This tactic of "code-switching to the extreme" leaves us with confused youth who are taught to pretend to have values of the middle-class and wealthy without the corresponding material benefits. Nothing exemplifies this strategy more than the popular work of Ruby Payne and her *Framework for Understanding Poverty* series. Widely popular several years ago in public schools serving low-income children in both urban and rural settings, the essence of Ruby Payne's work remains a core part of trainings offered to many administrators and teachers on how to understand and serve children who live in poverty. It is heavily laced with a conspicuous assimilationist perspective. According to Bomer, Dworin & Semingson, "many of Payne's representations of the daily lives of the poor emphasize depravity, perversity, or criminality; those who may not fit neatly into the dominant groups' ways of being are *defective, lacking in ability, and in need of being re-made* so as to better resemble those from the dominant classes (Bomer, Dworin, & Semingson, 2022)." Further, her program and "hidden rules of class" do not challenge the white and middle class privilege of educators but rather "legitimizes the stereotypes they carry into the classroom with them...that is why they are not intimidated; they relate to the hidden rules because the rules paint them as moralistically and intellectually superior to people in poverty (Gorski, 2008)." Gorski goes on further to argue that "what is infinitely more troubling than this simple reflection of capitalistic socialization is the extent to which supposed champions of educational equity and social justice have bought into her work (Gorski, 2008)." I have observed and experienced how the interplay of this assimilationist approach shows up specifically towards our black and brown boys, who sit at the crossroads of the intersection of race, class, and gender. They are seen as innately defective and lacking ability because of their race and personal or collective relationship to poverty. So, if we can dress them up, soften their voices, and teach them the soft skills, we increase their likelihood of acceptability. Despite the material success and popularity of men like Lebron James, Barack Obama, and Idris Alba, the assimilationist approach maintains that the goal is to not offend the sensibilities of white folks with our names, mannerisms, and very cultural being. This is when internal oppression is mislabeled "code-switching" as it requires our boys to hide, disappear, or deny their culture, rather than demanding/requiring that educators and those who serve young people become poly-lingual based on both culture and context. It renders cultural complexity and diversity inferior at best and worthless at worst. As my son, Sadiki, said recently: "I would have to bite my tongue until tasting the blood in my mouth."

The British form of colonialism, while operating with the same shared purpose of controlling the bodies and energy of their "subjects," acknowledged some value within the indigenous population and established structures and processes for them to achieve, but only so high. Under French rule, one had to 'become' French to possess the slightest value in society; under British rule, one's worth was predetermined through an unnamed yet politically enforced caste system. This "indirect rule" allowed a select few to increase their standard of living, albeit well-below their potential, without challenging the existing power structure of their liberal benefactors. Therefore, let us create opportunities for the native population to participate but not compete; to test, but not outperform. Does this sound familiar? We can clearly see here how this approach is rooted firmly in low expectations and outcomes, thereby developing an intense sense of learned helplessness and dependency, as described in Chapter One. Additionally, the inherent racism and bigotry of this perspective is evident in its narrow view of success and paths for success among our boys. We see this with all-night basketball community centers instead of STEM (Science, Technology, Engineering and Math) programs, barber career pathways in high school, but no active Black and Latino male recruitment in journalism or debate clubs. While I'm certainly not criticizing the spirit of support that many of these programs display, I do challenge the subtle (or not so subtle) paternalism evident as well.

Let us create opportunities for them to participate but not compete; to test, but not outperform.

Both approaches operationalize the belief that the answers for a community come from outside of that community and ultimately results in cultural abrogation. Additionally, it manifests in educators/adults normalizing low expectations, and creating limited paths to success and ultimately learned helplessness. Relying on current programs rooted in a colonial mindset, our boys of color will be stuck in a perpetual cycle of low achievement, disengagement, and economic instability.

Dr. Malik Muhammad

Patriarchal and Stereotypical Steel

As mentioned in Chapter One, programs rooted in stereotypical definitions of masculinity often harm our boys of color. Most often, these are individual or programmatic strategies designed to help adults connect with and relate to our boys. We often find well-intentioned practitioners encouraging Black and Latino boys as young as 10 to "man up" and "start taking on responsibility." This encouragement is admirable at times; it is also damaging. This premature urgency is a symptom of a larger fear: the lack of time. In the face of overwhelming odds and a brutal system that, according to Ta-Nehisi Coates, will "take your body," many assert that we don't have time to waste, that conditions mandate our boys grow up fast, despite their lack of biological, psychological, and emotional maturity. We want the bird to fly before it has wings. The critical flaw in this strategy is that we lean heavily towards the punitive approach as we attempt to temper the spirits of our boys into this patriarchal and stereotypical steel. I like this steel metaphor because it illustrates an important point. Steel, unbeknownst to most, is not a metal, it is an alloy, meaning that it is a man-made combination of at least two elements—iron and carbon. Iron and carbon are both natural elements and necessary for humans. However, steel is lauded for its density of composition (strength), limited corrosion (durability) and cost-effective versatility (usage). In the case of iron, it is more responsive to oxidation (sensitivity), bends with applied pressure (coping) and is best applied to specialized projects (personalization). By approaching our boys of color through a lens of tempering steel, we are going for the development of strength, durability, and utility (often on the playing field/court or battlefield), sacrificing their innate sensitivity, coping skills and personal humanity. **The "steeling" process makes our boys harder, 'stronger' and more resistant to a** harsh world. But it also results in them becoming less open, less able to communicate their feelings, and therefore more likely to internalize emotional pain. What's worse is that it communicates that this is how we make "men."

Equally oppressive, and perhaps more pernicious in its subtlety, is the de-masculinization of our boys of color. This is slightly different from the paternalistic approach mentioned above. The de-masculinization of Black and Latino boys is a reactionary response to patriarchal hyper-masculinity. It reasons that there is a deficiency within our boys of color and attempts to reimagine them as either androgynous or more feminine. While not always explicit, the strategy criticizes the "warrior" in boys of color as only aggressive, labels the bravado in their music and personal interactions as only chauvinistic, and mischaracterizes their unique display of emotion as numb. Our boys are recast as broken, half-beings who need only hugs and therapy. As we will discuss in Chapter Four, mental health supports are critical to helping our boys face and triumph through their emotional pain. However, strategies, programs and approaches that nullify their masculine dignity and attempt to remake them without honoring gender differences are oppressive and stigmatizing. This will also be addressed in Chapters Three and Four.

What's wrong with me Baba?

As just the two of us were driving away from home one day, my then 7-year-old son asked me a question that struck my soul. From the back seat, he asked: "what's wrong with me, Baba [father]." I looked in the rearview mirror to check him out and saw that he wore a face of profound sadness. "What do you mean Sadiki. What's going on?" It took some prodding, but he finally told me that while he was watching a "tearjerker" movie with his big sister, she started crying and then turned to him and said: "What's wrong with you...why aren't you crying? That's the problem with boys!" He loves and respects his sister more than anyone else, so he needed to know from me: what was wrong with him that he didn't cry at the sad part? I didn't know what to say at first. My 7-year- old son was struggling to reconcile the fact that his masculine self might express emotion differently and that was normal. We spent the next 45 minutes talking about how our "being boys" was both special and normal and that there are ways in which we, boys and men, are different and similar to girls and women. That nothing was wrong with him for not crying at the sad part. And that nothing was also wrong with me and his sister for always crying at the sad parts!

Dismissal

Dismissal of our boys' circumstances and needs, arguably, is one of the most detrimental approaches. This manifests in three distinct ways. The **first** is the outright rejection that schools and agencies have a responsibility to address the plight of our boys of color at all. This perspective is rooted in the racist over-simplification of research data as presented by "bell curve advocates." We won't take time here to disprove the 'findings' that suggest that our Black and Latino boys are inherently inferior to their white and female counterparts. Even moderate and non-progressive scholars have produced evidence that these findings are both false and racist. The **second** form of dismissal often comes from millionaire conservative apologists that dominate the microphone with their "pull yourself up by the bootstraps" mantras (i.e., Bill Cosby, Armstrong Williams, Ben Carson, and Bill O'Reilly). Their logic is as simplistic as it is perverse: boys of color, their families, and marginalized communities, in general, are solely responsible for their plight, and the very thought that anyone or anything shares responsibility is crippling. Indicative of a "blame the victim" and defend the system approach, it rejects the notion that we need supports and practices specifically designed for those suffering most and replaces them with stricter discipline, punishing parents/families, and glorifying the tiny number of those who "make it" like themselves. The **last** approach is the most challenging as it is the most widespread. This third form of dismissal acknowledges the data and understands that something is going on with our boys of color, however, it stops short of accepting responsibility to do anything about it. This comes from both an acceptance of the racist idea of "colorblindness" and ultimately a lack of courage to take a stand for our boys.[10] When we hear educators say that they just treat their boys of color like everyone else or that if we focus on this population, it is discriminatory, we are hearing the implied strategy of dismissal, and our boys are on the receiving end of it.

The message communicates that our boys of color don't warrant special attention and reinforces the defeatist idea that our boys are not worth it--the time, the energy, and the effort. To acknowledge that special attention is needed, we would have to acknowledge our role and responsibility in their plight and ultimately realign resources currently used only for the youth we identify with or value. Perhaps it will take courage to realize that we actually have been negatively

---

[10] It has been well established that "colorblind" ideology is actually a form of racism and upholds structural racism. Check out Monnica T. Williams' "Colorblind ideology is a form of racism" (Psychology Today, 12/27/2011) and Maia Niguel Hoskin's "Color-blindness perpetuates structural racism" (Forbes, 9/28/2022).

focusing on these young men while pretending to "treat them the same as other students." This book argues that we must positively, intentionally, and courageously focus on our boys of color.

How Treating Them the Same Meant Treating Them Differently...

When school reform advocates in school districts across the US began pushing for discipline consistencies through clear-cut Codes of Conduct, they perhaps inadvertently joined ranks with the zero tolerance demagogues. The results were discipline codes that districts and their legal teams could point to as being "fair, firm and consistent," a slogan which plays well to their middle-class tax base but was anything but fair for our boys of color. The implicit and explicit racial and gender bias of building and district-level administrators manifested itself in disproportionate use of punishments and school exclusion for discretionary offenses like class disruption and insubordination. As districts purported to have policies that were race, gender, and ability *neutral* and school cultures that were *inclusive*, the data clearly shows that they were *biased* against Black and Latino boys who were *excluded* more often than anyone else.

Single cure approaches

In many schools and districts, there might be an initiative to mentor young men of color <u>or</u> increase their participation in STEM programs <u>or</u> launch hip-hop oriented math clubs <u>or</u> 'Boys Read Too' programs with culturally and age-relevant literature for boys of color. These programs are often championed by a progressive educator and funded by a time-limited grant in partnership with a local university or national foundation. This approach is precisely why they fail. First, the initiative lives and dies on the shoulders of a lone champion in the school or district. Perhaps they have positional authority and wield resources now, but their tenure in the district is not perennial, and the programs often die when they leave their position or the district. This has been my experience with programs I have both launched and watched die when I left. Secondly, relying on external funding sources is obviously problematic. Frankly, if the conditions that have created our current situation facing our boys of color are within the core of our institutions, the funding to repair and restore our boys should also come from the core resources of our institutions. Our boys are not failing and struggling due to the presence or lack of external funding, therefore let us reject the idea that their solutions rely on external

> **Frankly, if the conditions that have created our current situation facing our boys of color are within the core of our institutions, the funding to repair and restore our boys should also come from the core resources of our institutions.**

Dr. Malik Muhammad

funding as well. Lastly, these initiatives fail because we did this program *or* that program. This apple or orange approach leaves our hopes resting on a single cure and a single person. The bandwidth of the lone champion pushing an initiative is finite. No one person has the resources and energy to launch several initiatives simultaneously.

Additionally, there is a problematic relationship with research and running comprehensive initiatives. I believe that:

- there is an incessant need to research all practices within a narrow academic framework designed more for contributions to articles and the research community than to the immediate implementation to save the lives of our boys of color.
- the need to be considered "research-based" or "evidenced-based" overrides the need to be practiced and field-based. I love the concept of Practice-Based-Evidence.[11]
- Most often, the design, purpose, and content of the research methodology conflict with issues of confounding variables and generalizability, which limit the roll-out of comprehensive programs, including several initiatives simultaneously.

In the final analysis, we need to place an "AND" instead of "OR" between our programmatic initiatives.

---

[11]From Bartgis & Bigfoot, 2010: "Practice-Based-Evidence (PBE) is becoming common language and represents practices that come from the local community. PBEs are embedded in the culture, are accepted as effective by local communities, and support healing of youth and families from a cultural framework (Isaacs, Huang, Hernandez, & Echo-Hawk, 2005). Many of these PBE have been in place for years and for many tribal communities, for centuries.

A Powerful Analogy

To drive home this point clearly, let us introduce here an important analogy: cancer treatment. There is no single cure for cancer; however, oncologists will explain that with the right combination of interventions, including early detection, chemotherapy, radiation, surgery, diet/exercise, support systems, and a positive attitude, they can effectively create a cure for cancer. Cancer rates are falling, not because of one single magic pill, but because of a combination of effective therapies together, a national consensus that it is an epidemic, and a $7.3 billion dollar budget to research the problem (National Cancer Institute 2023). For the epidemic of the chronic failure of boys of color, I argue that it is the same: there is no single cure for the problem, but we can identify a combination of effective strategies that together might lead us towards curing the epidemic facing them and this work. These curative "practices" need to be innovative, challenge our mindsets and current assumptions, and be implementable within the places that the masses of our boys find themselves: public schools and in our communities. My work has led us to identify six of these practices, which, when taken together, form the framework for the comprehensive approach put forward in this book and part 2. These six practices are:

1. Single-gender environments
2. Mental health supports
3. Restorative practices
4. Rites of passage
5. Innovative mentoring
6. Activism and Self-Discipline

Each practice, rooted in our implementation and experience within the traditional public and alternative school contexts, contributes to the synergy of a comprehensive plan for saving our boys. I agree with Larry Davis when he asserted that the services for our boys of color must be targeted, comprehensive, coordinated and integrated, as well as locally planned and directed (Davis, 1998). These practices represent what progressive environments have done and can do to produce a "medicinal cocktail" to save our boys of color. Let's imagine together how the synergy between all six can create a revolutionary treatment plan. Let's take these six, add a heaping $7.3 billion dollar budget, and save our boys of color in the morning!

In this book, Part One, we will explore the first three practices and set up the conversation for Part Two, where we explore the last three practices.

Reflection & Application

1. Reflect on the boys of color that you work with. Are there ways, subtle or explicit, that we privilege those who are a bit more culturally assimilated in how they speak, dress, or otherwise interact culturally? How might we as adults make them behave in ways that make it easier for us to relate to them culturally?

2. Consider the extremes of stereotypical steel and de-masculinization that our boys face. Name some messages in your environment that communicate both of these problematic approaches.

3. Which of these forms of dismissal do you see most prevalent within your own language and environment? What is the outcome of each?

Dismissal approaches	Outcomes
Let's face it, these boys of color are just inherent problems.	
The real problem is that they make excuses instead of just getting their act together.	
I don't see color, we need to just treat them like everyone else.	

4. Use the web below to identify the current initiatives and interventions specifically designed for your boys of color. Then draw lines to connect the initiatives with each other if they are engaged in co-planning, co-implementation, and attempt to work in harmony and synergy with each other. In my experience, most don't.

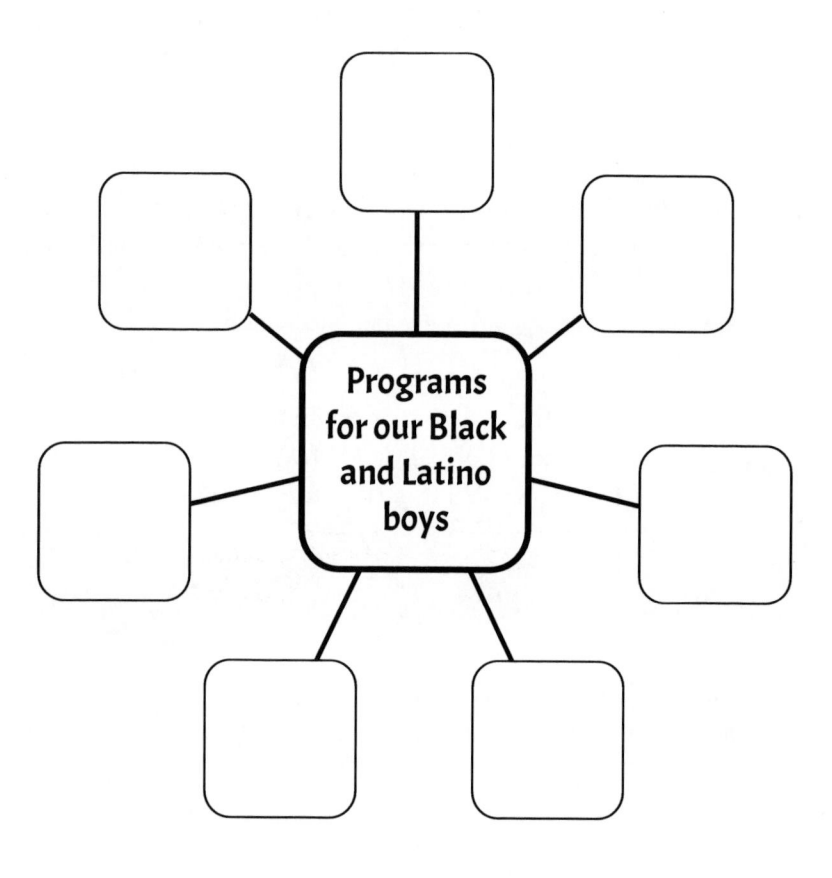

Programs for our Black and Latino boys

3

A Special Place for Our Boys: Single Gender Environments

> My other, my partner, I was teacher, he was father
> I skilled, he schooled, we chilled, we moved
> We thug, we hung, we ate, we slept
> We lived, we died, I stayed, you left
> Remember how we played to the left?
> And we stayed out of trouble 'cause we stayed to our self.
>
> Lil Wayne, "I Miss My Dawgs"

Let us start with the most controversial of our six practices: single-gender environments, particularly all-male classes, programs, and schools. Despite the controversy, the simple fact is that gender matters for our boys of color, and by extension for the communities that they come from. To argue that our boys should not have a specialized environment designed with them in mind is to dismiss their needs as discussed in the previous chapter. Our black and brown boys face unique challenges that specifically and dramatically affect them. As research shows, their educational and social experiences vary by gender within and across ethnic and racial groups (Hubbard & Datnow, 2005; NCES, 2009; Lee Jr. & Ransom, 2011).

If we concede that our boys' challenges and conditions are different, the most logical (and not at all radical) next step would be to differentiate our environments to improve their lot and to disallow the demagogues of "sameness" and "tradition" to win the day.

If we concede that our boys' challenges and conditions are different, the most logical (and not at all radical) next step would be to differentiate our environments to improve their lot and to disallow the demagogues of "sameness" and "tradition" to win the day.

I have profound respect for our brother and scholar Dr. Pedro Noguera, and while he is correct when he states that "there is no magic to be found in merely separating boys of color from their peers" (Noguera, 2012), there is another important point to consider. Single-gender schools and classrooms can provide the physical context, or milieu, to implement specialized interventions more easily. In short, single-gender schools and classrooms are the "intensive care units" needed to adequately launch targeted interventions for our boys of color.

Where are the single-gender environments and why do we need them for our boys of color?

As of this writing, in the U.S. there were approximately 1,100 single-gender environments for all students (about 60% of these were classrooms within coed public schools), representing a mere 1.1% of all public schools in the country. Two important conclusions emerge:

1) 98.9% of the outcome data indicating that boys of color are facing an educational crisis comes from their experience in coed environments, and

98.9% of the outcome data indicating that boys of color are facing an educational crisis comes from their experience in coed environments

2) Very little research exists on the impact and outcomes of single-gender environments for these boys, but the research that does exist is promising.

An important first question raised by proponents and critics alike is "why would we even consider a separate learning environment for our boys of color?" David Banks, founder of the Urban Prep Academy, a single-gender school for urban boys of color in Chicago, answered with: "they ask us why...as though what the boys are currently involved with is working" (Gewertz, 2007). Critics maintain that if we treat our boys of color more "the same" or provide them with even more or stronger doses of the current academic, social, and disciplinary interventions, then we will neutralize the discipline gap and the achievement gap. In their commitment to a version of "mainstreaming," these arguments advocate for little to no differentiation of interventions based on the needs of our boys of color. Differentiation can be likened to specialization and there are numerous examples of effective specialization that we can look to for guidance. In academia, business, government, and healthcare, environments are created and organized to focus primarily on one significant area or issue. Specialists are recruited and sufficient resources are dedicated to study and understand the nuances and subtleties of a phenomenon. Then interventions are developed and implemented based on cutting edge research. Like education departments for the development of teachers, repair shops for a certain German designed vehicle, or specialty hospitals for treating cancer, single-gender environments for boys of color provide the "intensive care units" needed to adequately launch targeted interventions for this population. They provide the milieu for a specialized focus to meet the needs of boys of color.

> **To argue that our boys should not have a special environment designed with them in mind is to participate in the same dismissive thinking that has caused their problems in the first place.**

What is the hope or promise of single-gender environments for our boys of color?

Single Gender environments specifically bring to the fore conversations around the intersection of race, gender, and culture, which significantly influence the trajectories of these boys of color. Likewise, the debate around these classrooms makes educators and policymakers discuss these dynamics ourselves. On the practical level, single-gender environments allow us to incorporate critical, specialized support for our boys of color. In so doing, they produce their own set of positive experiences. In a comprehensive study of single-gender private schools, Riordan identified 12 potential positive effects of single-gender environments (Riordan, 2002). These include:

- diminished strength of negative youth cultural values,
- greater degree of order and control,
- provision of more successful role models,
- reduction of sex differences in curriculum and opportunities,
- reduction of sex bias in teacher-student interaction,
- reduction of sex stereotypes in peer interaction,
- provision of a greater number of leadership opportunities,
- single-gender schools require a pro-academic parent/student choice,
- smaller school size,
- emphasizing academic subjects taken by all students,

- positive relationships among teachers, parents, and students that lead to a shared value community with an emphasis on academics and equity, and
- active and constructivist teaching and learning.

Indeed, all students could benefit from these positive school experiences, especially our boys of color, although many they lie outside of the narrow, but popular metric of student achievement. According to Salomone, "if research on single-sex education addressed only educational outcomes related to gender equity, it would deny a wealth of knowledge that these programs potentially could offer the education of at-risk students. It also would have a chilling effect on educators and policymakers and dissuade them from testing this approach on the very students for whom it might hold dramatic benefits—minority boys" (Salomone, 2006).

In environments specifically designed for boys of color, the complexities of race, gender, and culture can be overtly and directly addressed. We can speak 'truth to power' about the intersection of these critical and determinant factors within this safe haven for boys of color. As we will explore in more detail in Chapter Four, culture can be both an essential and protective factor in environments like these. Critical race theory researchers Mitchell and Stewart studied both the Urban Prep Academy in Chicago and Benjamin E. Mays Institute in Hartford, CT. They found that race and culture were "re-conceptualized and experienced by students, parents, teachers, and community members in empowering ways and relationships that made developing resiliency more possible and academic success more achievable (Mitchell & Stewart, 2013)."

A Site of Resiliency

In single-gender environments, we can be explicit and deliberate in implementing culturally relevant interventions. As one researcher noted in his findings about a school for boys of color in the U.S. South:

> "I learned that students and teachers developed an eighth [Nguzo Saba] value in response to quitting, "Never Quit." The "Never Quit" value emerged in direct response to *expectations overload,* which affected both the efforts of teachers and students as they encountered social and academic complexities. Each of the seven Kwanzaa values are typically taught to children in their Swahili form. *Imani* for instance is Swahili for faith, but there is no direct translation to Swahili for "Never Quit." However, the Swahili noun *imara* means perseverance, endurance, power, or strength. Here *imara* is defined as the power to persevere, and it captures the combined efforts of families, teachers, and students as they pursued success together, despite the complexities that they encountered along the way (James, 2010)"

Asset and strengths-based approaches, which are gaining traction among educators, help challenge the negative cultural labels of "at-risk" and "deficient" prevalent in traditional research about this population. These approaches are deeply rooted in the resiliency perspective, which can be viewed in two ways. First, resiliency for boys of color (and others) is seen as an individual phenomenon, a positive adaptation to adverse life circumstances. From this perspective, specialized environments for boys of color are not required, as success is based on individual effort. However, here the behaviors, values and cultures of white children and communities are positioned as the normative standard against which all other cultures and communities are judged (Boyden, 2005) and the resilient boy of color is described as someone who can assimilate white middle-class values (James, 2010). It is within this context that we hear about the popular notion of grit for our Black and Latino youth.

In his criticism of this approach, James states that "success must be re-conceptualized as a contested reality for African American males, not as a given outcome resulting solely from individual effort; [we must understand] how urban African American males can matriculate in a society that resists their advancement...this requires more than a slippery notion of individual success." Dr. Yasser Payne is also critical of this approach. He argues that "this model does not adequately connect the responsibilities of the community or the effects of larger social structures (e.g., government, education, police harassment, economy, family, etc.) to the development of the individual's agency and/or presumed "nonagency." (Payne Y. , 2011)

A second, and alternate perspective, is shared by ecological resiliency theorists who conceptualize resiliency as deriving from interactions between individuals, communities, families, and institutions. They argue that these interactions develop, deepen, and positively "orient" resiliency toward success for boys of color. Specialized environments for boys of color can build resiliency by leveraging relationships with authentic caring adults who consciously commit to serve this population (Hubbard & Datnow, 2005). Moreover, studies show that students receive the most support and elicit the highest expectations from educators when there is a high degree of overlap in values and norms between the two groups (Mehan, 1996; Stanton-Salazar & Dornbusch, 1995). Some have suggested that this overlap is most likely to occur when students and their teachers are from the

The Problem with Grit

I'm a true believer in the concept of perseverance and resiliency, support the work of Dr. Angela Duckworth, especially when combined with Dr. Carol Dweck's concept of a growth mindset. However, without an included analysis of oppression, we run the risk of grit being possibly a metric of how good one suffers well. How well you can "**grin and bear it**". For many of my students, mostly boys of color, they have demonstrated a sensitivity to oppressive school systems, unconsciously rebelling against them through disruptive behavior and poor academic performance. They have not shown a proclivity to persevere in the face of these adverse school conditions. However, once we have curated spaces for the volume to decrease and really see them, they have leveraged their survival strengths from living as a black or brown boy in this society towards doing better academically and in relationships with adults and each other. They come in with resiliency, our task is to clear some of the obstacles, so that they can 'show and prove' it on the remaining ones.

same socioeconomic class (Bourdieu, 1984; Lareau A. , 1989); or have a common "racial" or ethnic identity (Foster, 1991; Ladson-Billings, 1995; Lareau & Horvat, 1999). Gender matching or mismatching also can affect teacher-student interaction (McGrath & Sinclair, 2013).

Within a culturally and gender-relevant context, boys of color are not measured against white students, but rather, the positive and constructive aspects of their own culture are normalized so that they are measured against excellence in that standard. These same specialized environments can become "sites of resiliency." Payne defines this concept as "resiliency attained as a consequence of key ethnic and culturally based relationships with people in particular psychological and physical spaces, or "sites," [where] issues of trust, challenge, and confirmations of the [young] men's social meaning is addressed (Payne Y. , 2011)."

And how about the teachers?

Teachers familiar with single gender environments are overwhelmingly supportive of them. In one study (Speilhagen, 2011) of middle school teachers in single-gender classrooms, the majority of teachers who responded to the survey (87%) agreed that girls and boys process information differently and that single-gender classes allow the teachers to address the specific needs of each group. In addition, 61% of the teachers stated that both boys and girls seem comfortable with single-gender classes, while 68% of the teachers felt that there was greater participation by both girls and boys in single-sex classes. More teachers (71%) at the boys' academy stated that "the students are more focused and on-task in single-gender classes" than their counterparts in the coed academy (57%). Similarly, in the boys' academy, 82% of the teachers stated, "There is greater participation in single-gender classes," as compared to only 50% of teachers in the coed academy. Moreover, there was a significant increase in the response to whether single-gender classes should continue as an option, with 52% agreeing in the fall as compared to 94% of the teachers in agreement in the spring (Speilhagen, 2011).

In another two-year ethnographic study of low-income and minority students attending experimental single-gender schools in California from 1998-2000, teachers overwhelmingly felt that their students were in desperate need of what we now call social-emotional support. In many cases, the single-gender setting seemed particularly well positioned to address these needs. Teachers said that the absence of students of the opposite sex made it possible to have candid conversations that were essential to their students' well-being. The students affirmed this: "We can talk to them [teachers]," one girl said, and then continued, "They're not like the type of teacher that won't listen. They care about us, and we can talk to them about anything, and they won't say nothing" (Hubbard & Datnow, 2005).

Let's consider the doubts and criticisms

Despite the educational crisis facing many boys of color, we find hesitation to support single-gender environments on behalf of some educators. In fact, in two of my recent keynotes addressing a comprehensive plan for boys of color, most of the questions raised by the participants centered on the resistance anticipated with implementing single-gender environments. In my experience, the crux of the opposition, presented by organizations like the American Civil Liberties Union (ACLU) and the National Organization of Women (NOW), centers on questions of legality, equity, and fairness. However, back in 2007, the U.S. Congress eased federal regulations to allow for grouping by gender based on several conditions, including the existence of a compelling state interest based on improving the achievement of students, providing diverse educational opportunities, or meeting the needs of particular students (Gewertz, 2007). For most observers, the current plight facing boys of color clearly reaches the legal threshold of a compelling state interest. **We must ask ourselves: is the plight of our boys of color a compelling state interest because of their failure is or due to it?**

> **Sixty years of coed and integrated education have developed their own set of racist and implicit biases based on the current academic and discipline gap between boys of color and white females.**

The ACLU currently has an active campaign against single-gender environments. In their position paper, "Why Single-Sex Public Education is a Civil Rights Issue," they argue that single-gender environments for boys of color harken back to the Brown v Board of Education days, where integrated schools separated black boys away from white girls based on the belief that these boys were sexually out of control predators in the presence of white girls (ACLU, Why Single-Sex Public Education is a Civil Rights Issue, 2014). In the Jim Crow era, schools for Black people were usually not segregated by sex, because white legislatures did not care much about the possible corruption of black girls (Balkin, 2002). While compelling in its emotional appeal, sixty years of coed and integrated education have developed their own set of racist and implicit biases as demonstrated by the current academic and discipline gap between boys of color and white females. This issue, therefore, continues the necessary conversation around serving all students' needs and creates a tension in interpreting civil rights or equality of education.

The ACLU and NOW have framed single-gender environments for boys of color as unlawful, asserting that they are discriminatory against girls and low-income white students, promote sex stereotypes, and legitimize institutional sexism (ACLU, Why Single-Sex Public Education is a Civil Rights Issue, 2014). Some opponents have argued that the only just and persuasive reason for single-gender environments would be to address past discrimination against girls. In response to this, Salomone writes:

"That view, however, not only misreads the law but it is also severely outdated and defies recent findings on gender and schooling. We now understand that gender equity, neutrally defined, cuts both ways on a wide range of social and academic indicators...Even those of us who feel passionately about women's equity must recognize a simple fact: while girls still have difficulty reaching the top of the academic achievement ladder, especially on standardized tests, or moving into certain science-based careers, these realities pale in comparison to the escalating academic downslide that has harmed many boys of color in its reach. And so, it is reasonable to conclude that single-sex programs for boys of color also fit under the umbrella of gender equity loosened from its mooring to intentional discrimination." (Salomone, 2006)

Put more plainly, "criticisms of discrimination [of single-gender environments for boys of color] are intellectually dishonest because we already segregate based on race and SES now in reality" (Gewertz, 2007; ASCD, 2013). Consciously creating specialized environments for our boys of color is far more beneficial than leaving them in their current racially and economically segregated (by zoning and feeder patterns) environments. To some extent, the same arguments against affirmative action and unemployment programs are being used by opponents of single-gender environments to label them as unfair and discriminatory. In fact, the ACLU's own rebuttal against affirmation action opponents can be applied to single-gender environments:

Indeed, the argument that affirmative action **[insert single-gender environments here]** is "unfair" suggests that without such programs, everyone, including women and people of color **[insert boys of color]**, would be treated equally. Not even the most optimistic – or misguided – observer of our nation's history or contemporary society could make that claim in good faith (ACLU, Affirmative Action - ACLU Position Paper, 2000).

Given the overwhelming data which shows that outcomes differ so blatantly based on race and gender within their current coed environments to the detriment of boys of color, it appears hypocritical and disserving to refuse targeted alternatives for this population. Using specialized environments to meet the needs of children is common but the determination to implement them for our boys of color is unfortunately, lagging. In recent conversations, I've begun challenging those who oppose single-gender and specialized environments for boys of color. I ask: If funding is freely awarded for specialized hospitals like the Veteran's Hospital or Cancer Treatment centers, if we can see that need requires differentiation and specialization in key areas of our lives, how can we not apply this same life-saving logic to our boys of color?

Given the overwhelming data which shows that outcomes differ so blatantly based on race and gender within their current coed environments to the detriment of boys of color, it appears hypocritical and disserving to refuse targeted alternatives for our boys of color.

The Practical Application and Challenges to Implementation

The Prestige Academy, in Wilmington, Delaware, was a single-gender middle school specifically designed for boys of color. For four years, our family drove across two school district feeder patterns, past several elite private schools so that our son could attend this special place, built with him and his classmates in mind. The founder of Prestige is Dr. Jack Perry, a friend, colleague, and fellow champion for boys of color. I interviewed Dr. Perry about the practical application and challenges of building these environments. You can find our interview at **https://akobenllc.org/wecansaveourboysofcolor/**. From this discussion and my own experience, these are recommendations for implementation:

Start small

Often, what we need is the opportunity to launch a singular, small program, group, or class dedicated explicitly to our boys of color. We don't have to go for the full homeroom, wing of the building, or whole school at first. By starting small, we can understand the temperature within the environment, learn critical lessons (especially from the boys themselves) and build our own confidence and competence along the way.

Prepare for resistance

As we have identified in this chapter, not everyone believes that we need special places focusing on our boys of color. Plan for the questions and critiques around fairness, sameness, and segregation, even from progressives. Prepare with data around what is happening with our boys of color within your environment and lean into existing examples of differentiation within your systems (English Language Learners, honors/gifted and talented, etc.).

Look for models that have come before (they exist)

Programs, classrooms, and schools specifically designed for our boys of color have existed for over a half-century, with a wealth of lessons learned. Not much of what we will build will be totally innovative, but rather, will echo the hard work done before us by similar like-minded activists. Tap into powerful resources like the Coalition of Schools Educating Boys of Color (www.COSEBOC.org) for guidance and a village of support.

Incorporate rituals of bonding, celebration

As we will explore the practice of rites of passages in the next book, our boys need explicit moments to denote a transition from one phase to another. The Prestige Academy included many specific rituals, including the shirt and tie ceremony for incoming students. Students "transition" after their first week, having earned the right to now attend in their school uniform. Frequent public and private celebrations of victories of performance and engagement remind our boys that they belong here, in this special place, with these other special boys of color.

The family with our son, Sadiki, at his tie induction ceremony at Prestige Academy, 2010.

Encourage healthy competition

We should harness the intuitive power of competitiveness within many of our boys by directing that energy toward progress and excellence, primarily as part of the collective.

At Prestige, homerooms, named after the alma mater of their teachers, would compete in vocabulary battles, community service points, as well as in lacrosse tournaments. Leveraging their innate desire to push towards achievement and recognizing that too often they are not seen as achievers, we can direct that energy towards finding ways in which they can compete and win in the games that matter. We teach them not only how to be gracious winners, reflective in defeat, but also helping them remember that collective victory is always the priority over the individual win.

Think emotional as well as physical safety

When initiating single-gender environments for our boys, concerns about physical safety should not be at the top of our list. As we discussed in Chapter 1, the obsession with controlling the bodies of our black and brown boys is a predominant approach. Yes, we want them to feel and be safe with each other and us, but also, and primarily, to experience emotional safety. Time and again, we learn that by attending to emotional safety with emphasis, there are less requirements to focus on physical safety. Our special environments designed for our boys of color should be places where they can feel vulnerable to put down their constructed guards and emotional weapons of defense.

Reflection & Application

1. Given that this practice is the most controversial, why do you think that is? How did you initially feel about single gender environments prior to reading the chapter? How about now?

2. Out of the 12 positive outcomes from single-gender environments listed in this chapter, which 2-3 resonate with you most given the needs of the boys of color you work with directly?

3. In this chapter, we discussed different approaches to perseverance. Fill in the rest of the chart below and reflect on some of the characteristics of those approaches and the role of single gender environments.

Individual grit	Collectively developed resiliency
Often code for how well you fit into white cultural norms.	Rooted in the norms of the community to which you identify

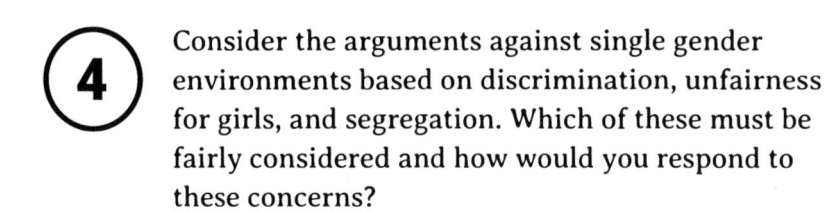

4. Consider the arguments against single gender environments based on discrimination, unfairness for girls, and segregation. Which of these must be fairly considered and how would you respond to these concerns?

5. Think about 1-2 of the implementation recommendations below. Consider how you might integrate these into an action plan for single gender environments for your boys of color:

- **Start small**
- **Prepare for resistance**
- **Look for models that came before**
- **Incorporate rituals of bonding & celebration**
- **Promote healthy competition**
- **Build emotional and physical safety**

Dr. Malik Muhammad

4

Healing Emotional Pain: Mental Health Supports

> **Dying inside but outside you're looking fearless.**
> *Tupac Shakur*

To be a black or brown boy or man in this society means to often feel crazy or insane. How do we maintain a positive self-image when the negative narrative is so pervasive and damaging? How do we foster beautiful relationships with girls and women when we are both the victims and perpetrators of patriarchal oppression? As Larry Davis puts it, our black and brown boys are required to develop in ways that are deemed "normal," but they are frequently required to do so in environments that are hostile to their efforts.

The statistics for homicide, suicide, or accidents are radically different for boys and girls. That is, boys die or are injured by personally avoidable events much more often than girls. This suggests that boys in general are typically under serious social pressure to take risks and incentivized to act in self-destructive ways. This is even more so for our black and brown boys, who are also more likely to be the victims and offenders of interpersonal violence. Community-based mental health practitioners have noted that the trauma, anxiety, and depression that black and brown boys face often go unaddressed due to institutional deficiencies and culture-based skepticism of mental health. The boys who most need the support of mental health interventions likely do not receive them primarily because we have not figured out how to push through barriers to access and relevancy.

Boys, in general, are typically under serious social pressure to take risks and incentivized to act in self-destructive ways.

If the experiences in both school and the community, not to mention factors like biology, parenting, and generational poverty, can create mental health challenges for our boys of

Dr. Malik Muhammad

color, what must we do to save their minds and emotional lives? This chapter seeks to address this question, explaining why we desperately need mental health supports for them, and what these might look like.

Unique Psychological Health factors for Black and Brown Boys

While we outlined many of the devastating effects of school and the community on the psyche of our black and brown boys in Chapter One, we excluded the effect on the psychological health of this population. These include disproportionate diagnoses, reactive masculinity, emotional concealment, sexual trauma, and hostile attributional bias.

Disproportionate Diagnoses

The data shows us clearly that too often the mental health establishment has not effectively served our Black and Latino boys:

- They are disproportionately diagnosed with both mild and severe mental illness.
- They disproportionately experience suicide, self-harm, and aggressive acts.
- They are disproportionately prescribed higher "doses" of traditional medicines and subject to most restrictive interventions like institutionalization, isolation, and special education.

This is what many of us parents of black and brown boys and concerned activists have been railing against for nearly 40 years and what widens the gap of cultural mistrust of mental health services and providers. Educators and parents alike have seen how Ritalin, Adderall, Concerta, Focalin and other drugs have turned normally gregarious boys into zombies barely able to stay awake. They have participated in IEP and manifestation meetings where school psychologists dispassionately read the results of diagnostic assessments and conclude that a 7-year-old boy has Oppositional Defiance Disorder. Many of our beautiful boys have been oppressively over-medicated and aggressively isolated by a system which neither values their culturally diverse modes of expression nor understand their instructional or disciplinary needs. Of course, this is not an indictment of medication to help support the biological or chemical needs of our boys, but **it is a condemnation of our biased mindsets that only see our boys as something that needs to be fixed, controlled, or quieted down instead of understood and cared for.** I struggle here, because given the intense and harsh societal reality our black and brown boys face, AND the social requirement to develop normally, of course we should expect disproportionate mental health effects for them. We might be delusional ourselves to expect anything different! It seems inhumane to recognize the manifestation of their emotional pain and reaction to a dysfunctional environment and then label them as the disordered! However, even if we only had the most conscious and progressive therapists conduct assessments on our black and brown boys, thereby possibly limiting negative bias, is it likely that they will still show a higher likelihood towards mental illness because of the intensity of their environment against them. If we only change the measurement tool and not the conditions, then this is more than probable.

Dr. Malik Muhammad

Reactive Masculinity

In Chapter One we outlined the challenges of hypermasculinity, noting its reliance on intimidation and alpha male posturing. Additionally, according to several researchers, for marginalized men [and boys of color], masculine power can express in unhealthy forms because of the lack of traditional routes to success and achievement (Courtenay, 2000; Whitehead, 1997). For some brothers, "street-life," with its own set of norms, benefits, and risks, is adaptive in the absence of academic and economic resources (Payne, Starks, & Gibson, 2009). Our boys who grow into men of color are born into a patriarchal society but are economically and socially marginalized and do not have access to the white male power and economic structure. In the quest to achieve a semblance of masculine power, in a society which prioritizes it above all else, black and brown boys are often likely to manifest forms of masculinity detrimental to their health and that of their community. Embedded in this reactive masculinity is the oppression and denigration of women, especially women and girls of color. To achieve just an inkling of superficial masculine dignity, we turn our words, hands and power against our sisters, daughters, wives, significant others, and each other.

Cost of Emotional Concealment

In nature, it is safest for animals to hide their injuries, to conceal their pain, lest they are seen as the weakest of the pack and therefore a victim. For many of our black and brown boys, it goes beyond just this. For them, it is more than just an unwillingness to be vulnerable. When faced with very real and perceived threats within negative environments, not only is it not safe to openly share vulnerabilities, but as a form of protection and coping you conceal your challenges, weaknesses, and struggles. You project, or hope to at least, a physical and mental attitude of normalcy, stasis, and control.

That is, by engaging in emotional concealment, our boys of color are communicating that "everything is okay," even when it is not.

It's Nothing that I can't handle

Back in college, one of my closest friends was clearly struggling with an emotional issue. His affect and demeanor showed that he was anguishing about something. I asked him what was going on and he replied that "he was good." I pushed harder and harder, until eventually he replied, "It's nothing that I can't handle."

I wasn't armed then with the language and skills to push past this obstacle. His statement shut down the conversation and my opportunity to lend support or at least a caring ear. As we discussed this interaction years later, he admitted that his masculinity then required him to maintain the façade of control and normalcy, even when it was clear that it wasn't working.

How many times have our boys and men of color, including myself, pretended to be "handling it ourselves" when we couldn't or didn't need to go at it alone?

What is the psychological cost of this façade? What price do they pay for what Tupac so brilliantly put: *Dying inside but outside you're looking fearless?*[12] We can argue that our boys' premature deaths, suicide, diabetes, heart disease, homicides and at-risk behavior have as much, if not more, to do with the psychological costs of holding things in than to mental illness.

Sexual Abuse and Boys of Color

We project hypersexuality upon black and Latino boys, dehumanize their bodies through depersonalization, and reinforce the status of maleness within a patriarchal society without corresponding power. Within this context, for our boys who have experienced or survived sexual abuse, the impact is even that much more devastating.

Add, the "never ask, never tell, never think about" ethic and you have many sexually violated boys who become broken men who suffer with intense psychological, emotional, and soul pain. This pain shows up in clinical issues around feelings about self, feelings about others and feelings in relationships to others (Myrie & Schwab, 2023). Oprah Winfrey, in an important set of shows in her farewell season of 2010, spotlighted male victims of sexual abuse, especially men of color victimized as boys. There are no solid projections of the percentages of black and brown boys who experience childhood sexual assault, but there is consensus that the numbers are higher than reported. How does this inform our mental health supports to help them develop into healthy young men? How do their symptoms manifest and

---

[12]It is really important to note that this line comes from Tupac's "Keep Ya Head Up," and is referring to the struggles of women. My sister Malene Kai Bell reminded me that it is one of the few lines in hip-hop by a man that acknowledges Black women's pain. I use it here to also recognize that the façade is a common and terrible default for many of us.

what nuances exist compared to girls? We need interventions that help them heal both their sense of self and dignity and point towards what healthy manhood looks and feels like.

Hostile Attributional Bias

For some of our boys of color, they perceive more hostility in other people's behavior than is actually directed at them. This social perception deficit is common in marginalized people and is called hostile attributional bias. It demands real and perceived slights to be met with reactive hostility and challenge. It also expands the range of "respect" required by others. In other words, the degree of required behavior deemed respectful (deference, acknowledgement, validation) for us to be in community together increases in order for me to just trust that you are not an enemy. You gotta look me in the eye, but not in that way; you gotta say my name correctly, but not with that tone; you gotta acknowledge me, but not call me out.

Almost always, for our black and brown boys, this is misinterpreted by adults as defiance and aggression and met with punishment and pain or diagnosed as Oppositional Defiance Disorder. Yet, what we understand about trauma is that it affects the architecture of the brain, highlighting the mid-brain at the location of the amygdala, responsible for much of our emotional center points and survival responses. We are constantly scanning our environment for danger, sometimes misrecognizing an action as threat at times. Research has shown an association between trauma, anger, and aggression through social information processing mechanisms (Taft & Creech, 2017). What I have described in Chapter 1 more than suggests that the experience of our black and brown boys in school and in their communities is traumatic at times. Therefore, we should expect to see more of our boys adopt a survival response which looks like a hostile attributional bias where they see danger and ill-intent, even when it isn't present at the moment.

The Particular Challenges of Mental Health Supports and Boys of Color

Despite the relative lack of research into the mental health differences facing men and women of color, there is some evidence to suggest variances, especially in coping. According to Ward et al, "disregarding gender and age ignores within-group diversity and can have critical implications for documenting and understanding prevalence, treatment-seeking behaviors, and the potential need for gender- and age-specific treatment" between boys/men and girls/women of color (Ward, Witlshire, Detry, & Brown, 2013). Does the same hold true for boys of color and others? Our experience in working with black and Latino boys indicates that it does. While other youth might evidence similar coping mechanisms, we have found that the following issues frequently challenge practitioners attending to the mental health needs of boys of color.

Trust and cultural mistrust

Our boys' lack of interpersonal trust and cultural mistrust of professionals to have positive intentions in helping them is often misunderstood and misdiagnosed as a mild form of paranoia. For those of us who have any historical or contemporary understanding of how "professionals" and others have wielded "supports" to abuse and terrorize black and brown minds and bodies, we call this a healthy level of skepticism and rational fear. It reminds me of Oprah's interview with Dave Chappelle after he departed from television and was rumored to have had a "breakdown." In response to a question, Chappelle asked Oprah, "What is a black man without his paranoia intact?"

Several researchers (Franklin, 1999; Whaley & Davis, 2007) have found that both boys and men of color typically avoid mental health services because they do not believe that providers will understand their unique challenges. The issue of trust seems to be particularly problematic in interracial therapeutic encounters. However, it can also impact the connection and outcomes with female counselors and therapists. Davis (1998) perfectly states:

> No other group is as likely to be provided services by those who "differ" from themselves. Rarely can they expect to receive health, mental health, educational, or employment services from those of the same race, gender, or class. On the contrary, they are often helped by those who have had little exposure to them and even less practice experience with them. (Davis, 1998)

Our boys, who command a different set of vocabulary to express themselves, might simply say: "Who are you to tell me anything? You don't even know me! You don't know what I'm about!" Of course, the "knowing" them here is not just about having personal knowledge of their individual reality, but understanding the essence of who they are, their worldview and the tribe to which they belong. After all, why would we expect the most hardened, uber-masculine, socially misunderstood boys to be vulnerable for us if we have not put in the work to gain their trust through connection?

Why would we expect the most hardened, uber-masculine, socially misunderstood boys to be vulnerable for us if we have not put in the work to gain their trust through connection?

Outgrow it like Asthma

"Ain't nothing wrong with that boy, he just misses his Daddy!" I remember these words vividly, although Ms. Johnson spoke them almost 20 years ago during a parent conference about the behavior of her 9-year-old grandson, Frank. He had been fighting, screaming, and was physically restrained twice in the previous week. I looked at the boy's face at that moment and saw him wince in deep emotional pain as his deceased father was mentioned. I struggled to understand what Ms. Johnson meant, especially given that I could identify with Frank's wince. I still had that same reaction, even then in my mid-twenties, when I thought about my mother's death 6 years prior. On one level, Ms. Johnson was downplaying Frank's trauma and associated behaviors. She was not allowing emotional space, and therefore support, for Frank to explore his pain and experiences, and learn the positive coping skills needed to save himself now and in the future. Instead, she might have been doubling down on society's expectations that males, even 9-year-old versions of them, should just get over it. Expect pain and suffering, and "man up, you'll be alright."

However, Ms. Johnson was also asserting, in her own language, that her black grandson was suffering from an event-based experience and doesn't have sustained and pervasive mental health issues. *He misses his Daddy;* **therefore, he is acting up.** Implying, there is nothing clinically or diagnostically wrong with him. Put that way, her statement can be interpreted as both empowering and perhaps trauma informed. She expressed, to the point of pleading with the decision-makers in her grandson's school, that he will outgrow this behavior and mental state. Just like asthma!

Our son was diagnosed with asthma shortly after his first birthday. Over the next 5 years, this adventure included oxygen tents, running during lunch break to administer nebulizer treatments at his daycare, asthma pumps, back-up asthma pumps, and eventually self-regulation breathing techniques during time-outs on the football field. He matured beyond the limiting effects of asthma, but only through clinical interventions *and* coping skills. We had no idea at one year old if he would suffer from asthma throughout his life, but we wanted him to be treated like a normal, healthy kid. Like Ms. Johnson, I could see myself asserting to his football coach: "He'll be alright, coach. He just has asthma."

One challenge mental health practitioners face are caretakers, and sometimes the boys themselves, who will acknowledge that there is something wrong but profess the young 'men' can handle it; *it's just something they are going through*. This nullifies the need for intervention and support in their mind (Anglin, Alberti, Link, & Phelan, 2008)

I ain't really thinking about that

Some of our black and Latino boys and their families only see a psychological issue as a problem when it impairs basic functioning. However, what happens when "basic functioning" means the ability to effectively operate in survival mode?

By the time the trauma impedes the basic functions of taking care of themselves or interfacing appropriately with others around them, it is often way beyond when help was needed. We find some young men saying "I ain't really thinking about that," when asked about an adverse childhood experience (see Chapter One). Meaning that "my experience with sexual abuse, dysfunctional family, community violence and institutional racism" doesn't really impact my behavior or affect me. I've heard that trauma is like carbon monoxide; we only think about it when we feel its effects... [It is] silent but deadly. A challenge for providing mental health support for our boys of color is in the acknowledgement that there is an issue impacting them, and that the issue is not something they can ignore or "outgrow" without supports and interventions. To be clear, we must teach *and* value our boys enough to raise the bar on their well-being and mental health. We have to teach and show them that they deserve more than just survival, so that they are empowered to identify their emotional pain and can acknowledge that something has impacted them, that they are not made of stone, that they are human. But, *before we teach them,* we must change the way that we view them. We must abandon the harmful lenses upon which we view our boys, and the dismissive language of dehumanization that says, 'he should know, he'll be alright."

There is nothing wrong with my mind!

"Malik, he kept cussing and cussing…and my daughter was right there man!" That is what my friend said with an exasperated tone when he was describing a recent incident. He was in Ghana with his family on their first trip to the Motherland. They were all excited and having a great time when the driver of their tour kept cursing in front of his small daughter. At first, he tried to ignore it, but soon he approached the guy and said "Brother, are you crazy? Why are you cussing in front of my family. You need to stop!" That's when the most interesting thing happened. The driver was shocked, confused and upset. Not at being told to stop cursing, but by being called "crazy." He demanded that my friend take back his accusation. Through his frustration, the driver kept arguing that "there is nothing wrong with my mind." Finally, my friend said "Fine, you're not crazy, but asshole, you need to stop cussing in front of my family now!" The driver just nodded his head, apologized for using profanity and shook his hand.

For many of us, we would rather be anything, even an asshole, than be "crazy" or have a mental health issue.

Relying on the Barbershop

When black and Latino men struggle with issues related to parenting, relationships, and employment that affects our mental state, often our social conditioning of masculinity prevents us from seeking support. However, when we do, in whatever form, it is almost always to our informal network of close male friends and significant male relatives because the bond of commonality fosters a sense of trust. Sometimes this collectively takes place in men's retreats associated with churches, mosques, and fraternities. Other times, it is through what is shared and listened to at the barbershop. As many of us know, beyond the nonsense of sports debates and one brother wanting to assert the existence of UFO's, occasionally, the barbershop conversation touches on meaningful dialogue around positive fatherhood and the struggles of being a black or brown man in America. Our boys of color are not different. While they don't always have the barbershop or organized men's retreats, they do find moments between video games and joking about girls to talk about their frustrations with life, their parents, school, the police. When we see them walking together, standing in a circle, sharing their inner thoughts through rhyme in a cipher, this is part of their emotional release. The challenge here is that it is too often swayed by bravado, self-concealment of emotional pain, and seeking advice from others struggling with their own unresolved pain who cannot help beyond listening. We need to capture the informal nature of these trust-building relationships, expand beyond them to include skilled adults and provide more mental health skills for peer-to-peer work. This is what we are seeing with the Confess Project (www.theconfessprojectofamerica.org), which hails itself as "America's First Mental Health Barbershop Movement." Starting in 2016, it has grown to train 1,000 barbers annually to become mental health advocates. We need to build on movements like this as well as strengthen formal existing mental health services to better serve our boys of color.

The Challenge of Openness

When we combine the issue of cultural mistrust with the perception that mental health issues are to be ignored or outgrown, and the overreliance on the informal network of friends and relatives, we get to the ultimate and real challenge of psychological openness for our boys of color. The kind of disclosures that are necessary for healing and transformation requires an increasing level of vulnerability. As we noted, reactive masculinity requires our boys to be the hardest alpha male, therefore, there is no room for vulnerability, perceived weakness, or expression of emotional distress. The outgrowth of ascribing to this is that if we do see their vulnerability, weaknesses and emotional distress, we ignore it, mislabel it, or encourage our boys to just communicate it through their behavioral vocabulary (see Chapter One). Aggression, disengagement, playing small, hyper-masculinity are manifestations of their emotional selves. It is through wielding affective language, as we will discuss in Chapter 5, that we build their emotional vocabulary and strengthen our capacity to be vulnerable. However, in the absence of those skills, when our boys of color do "participate" in mental health services, individually or in a group, they may present as disengaged. We see stoicism and self-concealment. They are often wary of "genuine talk," which exposes uncharacteristic emotions, immobility, struggle with weaknesses, or lack of knowledge (Davis, 1998). This immobility, being stuck in place with only the opportunity to release emotional energy through talking, is so characteristic of many mental health programs. Sitting and talking, being vulnerable and comfortable with emotional dialogue is often out of sync with natural patterns of masculine interactions. That is not to criticize the importance of this method, rather, it names its exclusivity as a limitation. As such, it operates as a barrier to psychological openness with our boys of color. We'll explore the importance of integrating movement into this work further in this chapter.

The Power of a School-Based Mental Health Program for our Boys of Color

In the alternative schools we operate in Delaware through Transforming Lives Inc., we speak of our work as a marriage between education and mental health. Our approach is founded on the idea that a student's maladaptive school behavior is most often connected to internalizing symptoms (i.e., depression, anxiety, PTSD) that have gone unaddressed. As such, in the spring of 2014 we began using the Symptoms and Functioning Severity Scale (SFSS) to assess and monitor our students' behavioral health progress over time.

Administered by the clinician or school counselor and, if possible, completed by the youth and caregivers, the SFSS is given at intake into our program to establish a baseline score, followed by every marking period, and at transition. The SFSS is best considered a global measure of severity, providing information about externalizing and internalizing symptoms. It is comparable to other existing clinical outcome measures but has the advantage of being short (it takes only five to seven minutes to complete) allowing for frequent assessment over time. Respondents who rate their (or the youth's) severity as high are indicating that the youth is experiencing behaviors or emotions that are causing problems in his or her life. When a youth (or adult caregiver or clinician) reports low severity, it indicates that the youth is experiencing few problem behaviors or emotions.[13]

Mental Health is the specific lens through which our programs/schools view interventions with our youth. As such, we implement mental health support for all students throughout all our programs. Through our embedded counselors and clinicians, we use various evidence-based mental health practices, including Aggression Replacement Therapy, Skillstreaming for the Adolescent Child, Trauma Informed Practices, "How Does Your Engine Run?," and Walk and Talk Therapy.

Our team conducted an analysis of mental health outcome data, derived from the Symptoms and Functioning Severity Scale, for all high school students at one alternative school in Delaware during the 2013-2014 school year. Given its relative representation of student demographics to the larger student body, 70 high school students were chosen to pilot this mental health assessment. The average SFSS score at intake for all students was 55.68, while the mean change in their last score reported was -8.22 or -.77 of a SD (t = 7.62, p < .01). This 15% reduction in symptom severity effectively

---

[13] The SFSS is a sound psychometric assessment. It consists of 32 items that rate how frequently within the last two weeks the youth experienced emotions or exhibited behaviors linked to typical mental health disorders among youths, including attention-deficit hyperactivity disorder, conduct or oppositional defiant disorder, depression, and anxiety. Frequency is rated 1, never; 2, hardly ever; 3, sometimes; 4, often; or 5, very often. A total severity scale score is created by a simple average of ratings for each youth if at least 85% of items are completed.

moved most of the high school students assessed from the medium to low severity levels. *Additionally, the largest demographic, boys of color entered the school at somewhat lower levels of severity than their counterparts, however, they surpassed gains made by black females and far outpaced gains made by our white male students.* **In other words, the emphasis on mental health had a greater positive impact for boys of color than any other group of students at the school!**

While mental health was at the heart of the approach to transforming behavior for all students at the school, the evaluation conducted represented the first opportunity to objectively analyze mental health outcomes using a psychometric assessment like the Symptoms and Functioning Severity Scale (SFSS). As mentioned previously, nearly all students showed decreases in their severity symptoms, especially boys of color. Not surprisingly, data suggest that the longer/greater the dose of the school-based mental health intervention, the greater the level of decreases in severity scores.

The Key Elements of Mental Health Supports for Boys of Color

Our boys of color need mental health support that are culturally *and* gender relevant. While the former is sometimes noted in the field, too often mental health practitioners may do not consider the importance of gender considerations in their work. In their landmark book on the mental health of boys, *Raising Cain,* psychologists Kindlon and Thompson assert that "we bristle when we hear destructive or disappointing boy behavior excused with "boys will be boys," when the truth of those words – boys will be boys – could instead be used to advance the understanding that boys struggle in uniquely male ways at times, and they need "boy-friendly," adult love, support, guidance [and therapies] to develop a broad range of emotional responses to life's challenges" (Thompson & Kindlon, 1999)

Based on our work and research across the field, culturally adaptive and gender considered interventions are most effective in improving mental health outcomes for boys of color. These interventions involve tailoring evidence-based practices to better meet the cultural needs and preferences of black and Latino boys. The following mental health supports appear to have the greatest impact on healing emotional pain and addressing the behavioral health needs of our boys of color.

- **Make it Collective**
- **Walk & Talk**
- **Relevancy/Rapport**
- **Culture & Identity**
- **Explain it to them**

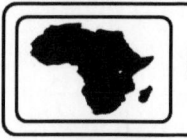

Make it Collective

Dr. Christina Watlington has been popularizing the notion that "**Hurt happens in relationships and healing happens in relationships.**" This is certainly true about our mental health interventions with our boys of color. Our experience has shown that we should default to providing these interventions within a collective setting, using the therapy group or support circle to be the main vehicle for healing. The social supports established by the collective allow for the work to continue beyond the 45 or 90 minutes in the circle together. This peer-to-peer work is precisely what they need.

Conducting these supports within a collective also accomplishes several other goals, described as curative factors by Larry Davis and most clearly benefits boys who have experienced trauma:

- **Universality:** Awareness that they are not alone. They have a shared experience with other boys like themselves. Helps to lessen feelings of deviance, isolation, and shame.

- **Instilling Hope:** Seeing others in the group getting better, resolving issues.

- **Group Cohesiveness:** Promoting positive group identity.

- **Interpersonal Learning:** Improve social skills, often hampered by effects of social isolation.

- **Catharsis:** Being able to emote, instead of holding it in. Express feelings of shame and outrage in an emotionally safe space

I would also add that mental health groups can:

- Approximate natural informal interaction they relate to outside of the healing space or circle.
- Provides an informal facilitator approach, deepening adult-youth relationships.
- Creates an exclusive and safe place for masculinity and vulnerability to coexist.

> **If they will continue to live in a community while coping with a mental health issue, then providing a micro-environment of safety, support and practice among their brothers makes sense.**

While some boys are dealing with a level of trauma or adaptive behaviors that make them contraindicated to participate in a mental health group or healing circle, joining the collective should always be the goal. If they will continue to live in a community while coping with a mental health issue, then providing a micro-environment of safety, support and practice among their brothers makes sense.

Walk and Talk

In our training workshop entitled "We Can Save Our Boys of Color,", I ask the men in the room to respond to a simple question: When you are really struggling with an emotional issue as a father, brother, or son, have any of you reached out to your friend and invited them over to talk it through with a glass of wine while sitting on the couch for three hours? Folks, both men and women, all seem to laugh, especially as most of the men call out a loud "NO"! I share that I've never done that either. When I'm struggling with an issue and I'm at a stuck point emotionally or need to vent,

I call up a good brother and extend the invitation – to go play billiards, workout, or grab a meal and watch the game. On the surface we are engaged in a physical activity, but on the subsurface we are unpacking the issue together. It starts with Connection before Content, as we always do as humans [more about this in *The Restorative Journey – Book One: The Theory and Application of Restorative Practices*], but our conversation eventually weaves to touch on many domains of our emotional lives as men: marriage, relationships, parenting, ailing parents, double consciousness, shame, and self-disappointment. All this while we are also trash-talking about making that shot or referencing old school hip hop. The movement and physical activity open us up. No one taught us this, we've just intuitively known.

Some may critique this as avoidant behavior and assert that the 'real work' comes when we are forced to sit down, be still and uncomfortable with the emotions as they come up; that the process of being vulnerable is too important to not embrace head on. I agree and encourage us to apply the BOTH/AND instead of EITHER/OR approach here. Being uncomfortable and vulnerable are critical requirements to address the emotional pain and issues our men and boys face AND we will not get them there if we don't acknowledge that they might approach these differently than women and girls.

Walk and talk therapy is not a new approach, but rather is a modern expression of what coaches, mentors and elders have done throughout history as we walked, climbed, and rode horseback together with our boys to help them open up.[14] It is a promising alternative that can provide a more comfortable and effective therapeutic environment for boys of color.

---

[14] For more on using movement in therapy, check out the brilliant Dr. Howard Stevenson's Playing with Anger as well as Cooley, Burns, & Cumming (2019) and Johnson, Singleton, & Brown, D. (2018)

Walk and talk therapy involves engaging in a physical activity like walking outdoors or playing a physical game with an adult or peers while engaging in a therapeutic conversation. This approach can be particularly effective for boys of color because it provides a more relaxed, informal setting for therapy, which can help reduce barriers to engagement and facilitate more open and honest communication. Walking side-by-side can also create a sense of equality and reduce power imbalances that can exist in traditional therapy settings. It feels right to say that the journey to manhood is done shoulder to shoulder, not face to face.

The journey to manhood is done shoulder to shoulder, not face to face.

Research has shown that walk and talk therapy can be particularly effective for black and brown boys. For example, Johnson and colleagues found that walk and talk therapy was associated with significant improvements in depression, anxiety, and stress symptoms among African American adolescents. The study also found that participants reported high levels of satisfaction with the therapy approach, and that an outdoor setting helped them feel more comfortable and engaged in therapy (Harper & Dobud, 2021)

Another study by Pickett and colleagues (2020) examined the experiences of black and brown boys who participated in walk and talk therapy and found that the boys reported feeling more comfortable and less stigmatized in the outdoor therapy setting, and that the therapy approach helped them build stronger relationships with their therapists. The boys also reported feeling empowered by the physical activity of walking, which helped them feel more in control of their mental health and well-being (Pickett, 2020)

In addition to these psychological benefits, walk and talk therapy can also provide physical health benefits that can be particularly important for boys of color who may face higher rates of physical health disparities. For example, another study found that walk and talk therapy was associated with significant improvements in cardiovascular fitness and physical activity levels among adolescent boys of color. The study also found that the boys reported feeling more motivated to engage in physical activity outside of therapy sessions (Cooley & Robertson, 2020).

Literally, taking a walk together accomplishes a few things with our boys. First, it activates the bodily-kinesthetic learning style that so many are naturally attracted to. Second, we go for the "shoulder to shoulder" instead of "face to face." This communicates that we are partnering in the healing journey, there is a give and take that must happen, with the heaviest ownership for the healing primarily being on the shoulders of who it belongs: the boy himself. Lastly, it helps counter the stigma of therapy by broadening the delivery – *we are just taking a walk.* Or playing a game, working out, or building something together.

Go for Relevancy and Rapport

The research and my experience are clear that providing mental health supports with gender and racial/ethnicity matching in mind is important. If we agree that establishing therapeutic rapport and alliance is paramount in the healing process, then we should acknowledge that gender, race, and ethnic relevancy are decisive factors. However, we see some of the same objections to these areas of relevancy as we do with single gender environments as discussed in chapter three.

Men of color with severe mental illness in a gender-matched therapeutic relationship reported significantly fewer paranoid symptoms than their counterparts in mixed-gender dyads during an assessment interview. Furthermore, "these findings also suggest that matching men [and boys] on gender and race may be more important for those who express a strong racial identity. Moreover, black mental health professionals high in racial consciousness may also be required for black and brown men with a strong racial identity. (Whaley & Davis, 2007)" Gender and race/ethnicity matching may help reduce the level of distrust of the mental health system "as these therapeutic encounters may be reminiscent of the male bonds that men of color experience in their communities (Cabral & Smith, 2011; Kivlighan, Drinane, Tao, Owen, & Ming Liu, 2019)."

While gender and race/ethnicity matching are important, we also need therapists to push beyond traditional relationships of therapeutic distance to establish a more informal connection with our black and Latino boys. Again, Larry Davis is instructive here, as he argues for a higher level of counselor self-disclosure in working with boys of color, given that trust, vulnerability, and rapport are so critical with this population. In short, if we are requiring them to get vulnerable, we must be willing to go first!

Our willingness to forthrightly answer direct, and often personal, questions about our lives increases credibility and promotes rapport. By sharing experiences which express genuine emotions and relating in a natural caring manner, we become a powerful role model for the boy. It enhances the boy's change process, not only by self-disclosing appropriate personal experiences but also by encouraging and affirming nontraditional masculine attitudes and roles.

Embrace Racial Identity and Culture as Coping

While we will spend more time exploring the curative factors of culture for our boys of color in the second book, it is important to connect the value of a positive racial identity and cultural self-esteem as significant mental health coping approaches for this population.

As previously described, racism and cultural bias significantly lace the physical and mental health of our black and Latino boys. As such, having a healthy understanding of race and culture is both amazing and protective for these boys. According to Gaylord-Harden, Burrow, et al (2012) in "A Cultural-Asset Framework for Investigating Successful Adaptation to Stress in African American Youth," racial identity has emerged as an important aspect of self that can contour responses to race-related stressors (Gaylord-Harden, Burrow, & Cunningham, 2012). Various studies[15] have shown that youth with high levels of racial identity are buffered from the ill effects of discrimination on subsequent levels of:

- depressive symptoms,
- perceived stress,
- psychological distress,
- academic performance and motivation,
- and behavior problems

Plainly speaking, the greater sense of racial identity and consciousness, the better able our black and brown boys can navigate a culture of racial and cultural discrimination.

For our boys, learning to successfully cope in an often hostile society is an important and normative process in their development. For instance, traditionally within black

---

[15]Check out Sellers, Caldwell, Schmeelk-Cone, & Zimmerman, 2003; Sellers et al., 2006; Wong et al., 2003

and LatinX communities we see two important culturally relevant coping strategies, including communalistic coping ("A brother is like one's shoulder" – Somali proverb) and spiritually-based coping. These are strategies based on a culturally centered worldview and grounded in the historical, cultural, and philosophical tradition of our communities.

One study found that culturally adapted cognitive behavioral therapy was more effective in reducing depressive symptoms among African American youth than standard cognitive behavioral therapy. The culturally adapted therapy involved incorporating cultural values, beliefs, and experiences into treatment, including discussions of racism and discrimination (Silveus, Schmit, Oliveira, & Hughes, 2023).

Another study found that a culturally adapted parent training program was effective in reducing behavioral problems among Latino youth. The program involved tailoring traditional parent training techniques to better meet the cultural needs and preferences of Latino families, including using examples and case studies that were relevant to their cultural experiences (Silveus, Schmit, Oliveira, & Hughes, 2023).

Lastly, a third study found that a culturally adapted family therapy program was effective in improving family functioning and reducing symptoms of depression and anxiety among African American families. The program involved incorporating cultural beliefs and practices into therapy, including discussions of spirituality, community, and family values (Silveus, Schmit, Oliveira, & Hughes, 2023).

Parents, communities, and religious institutions have, at varying degrees of success, attempted to transmit these cultural coping strategies to boys of color. Research has determined that a higher level of positive racial and cultural socialization embedded at home and from the community acts as a mitigating factor for these boys against substance use and the traumatic effects of exposure to community violence.[16] Again, to be clear, the more our boys are proud of their racial identity and culturally grounded, the less they are at risk of destruction by this society. The research is so strong, that we must weave and encourage racial and cultural socialization into our mental health work with our boys of color.

The research is clear: the more our boys are proud of their racial identity and culturally grounded, the less they are at risk of destruction by this society.

Use therapy to teach them how to understand themselves

One of the most powerful techniques that Dr. Christina Watlington teaches is the hand model of the brain. In her workshops, she dedicates a significant amount of time helping adults understand what is going on in the brain when it is impacted by traumatic events, including how the parts of the brain respond to survival, learning and restoration. She also does this same work with youth in therapy groups and individual sessions. What is so powerful here is that she is equipping the adults and youth with an understanding of what is really going on within themselves. They are not broken; they are not crazy. Instead, they are emotionally dysregulated due to heightened sensitivity to perceived harm or threat based on what happened to them. This is powerful

---

[16]Lots of good research here: Belgrave et al., 1994; Resnicow et al, 1999; Marsiglia, Kulis, & Hecht, 2001; Caldwell et al., 2004

because it is using therapy to teach, something that Dr. Watlington asserts is essential to good therapy. This changes the dynamic from therapy being something the clinician is doing TO or FOR the client, to psychoeducational therapy being something they do WITH the client. For our boys of color, empowering them with an understanding of what is happening with their brain as well as identifying their assets, internal and external resources, has shown to be helpful in supporting them with becoming unstuck and moving out of a state of desperation and limited options. We are arguing that counseling should be viewed as an educative process, with the primary focus being on teaching and the development of new skills or behaviors to deal more effectively with social and economic challenges. By doing so, we can show how mental health issues are problems to the extent that they impair normal daily functioning. If we can use therapy to teach what is going on within as well as skills to function well, then it may limit some of the stigma in getting help for our boys of color.

The Practical Application and Challenges to Implementation

I'm fortunate to have known and worked alongside a brilliant thought-leader and clinical psychologist, Dr. Duane Thomas, for the past two decades. His work as an academic, researcher and clinical practitioner has focused on serving the mental health needs of our Black and Latino boys. In a recent conversation with Dr. Thomas, we focused on several elements of practical application and challenges. Here are recommendations for implementation:

Reframe the resistance to therapy as protective coping:

In a very real sense, there is the valid belief by marginalized people that if I was to open up to someone and talk about some issues that I'm grappling with that the information may be misused in some kind of way. Our experience has been in working with our boys of color that there's an inclination towards, "How do I protect my family?" Even in some of the worst-case scenarios, there is still this need, desire, and deep cultural value to protect the family. So, the resistance to engagement might be protective coping against the possibility they will be displaced from family or their parents would lose rights.

Additionally, we must be careful to not pathologize the anxiety, worry, or fear by our black and brown boys about some misdeed that may occur from a service provider. It's self-protective to think that "Hey, I might have to be a bit more careful of what I'm going to share with this individual who's sitting in front of me who maybe comes from a different social group identity, because of a history of mistrust and abuse." It is our job to instill a sense of trust so they can start to feel safe enough to be vulnerable. We need to remember that the primary problem is not the suspicion. The primary problem is the conditions that created the suspicion in the first place.

Use informal networks as part of our holistic strategy:

Let's think of the barbershop or the wise, unyielding guidance from grandma as wrap-around support that can supplement and be incorporated within a larger plan of mental health services for our boys of color. These things shouldn't be mutually exclusive. Given some of the present challenges and the potential decline that some of our boys may face, we need a holistic and inclusive strategy that accesses, values, and appreciates these communities' strengths and

Our boys of color need the equivalent of mental health CPR, which can be delivered by any caring community member. At other times, they also need the equivalent of mental health surgery, therapy done by skilled professionals.

protective factors. What our boys need is the mental health version of community CPR where anybody can get down to help if needed. We need this support right now, the equivalent of layman's version of CPR. And other times they need the equivalent of sophisticated mental health 'surgery' conducted by qualified professionals who have training and years of experience to help heal the deep-seeded trauma and mental health challenges that lie underneath.

Get them moving and use the environment:

One of the most impactful stories Dr. Thomas told me from was early in his career as a psychologist, asking a supervisor "Listen, are there any rules of me actually taking my clients outside?" And the supervisor kind of sat there for a bit and he was like, "Uh, I guess not, I mean no one has ever asked to do that. I don't see a problem with it if the parent consents." Getting our boys' bodies and emotional vocabularies moving is an approach worth asking and fighting for.

Activate the expertise all around

When we are engaging in mental health supports with our boys of color, it must be a reciprocal educational process. We are perhaps the experts on evidence-based practices and frameworks, but they are the experts on themselves. No one has lived with and studied them longer or more deeply than they themselves. Let's involve them in not just the planning and treatment plan, but in expressing how they will both apply the strategy learned and teach another to do the same.

> **We are perhaps experts on evidence-based practices and frameworks, but they are the experts on themselves. No one has lived with and studied them longer or more deeply than they themselves.**

Reflection & Application

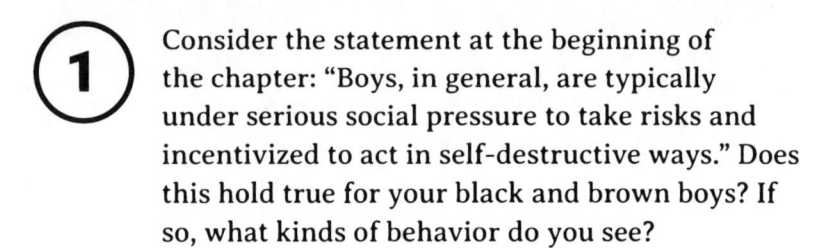

1. Consider the statement at the beginning of the chapter: "Boys, in general, are typically under serious social pressure to take risks and incentivized to act in self-destructive ways." Does this hold true for your black and brown boys? If so, what kinds of behavior do you see?

2. Provide real life examples for each of these psychological health factors facing our boys of color:

Disproportionate diagnosis	
Reactive masculinity	
Emotional concealment	
Hostile attributional bias	

3. How might you address the cultural mistrust of mental health providers by our boys of color?

4 How can the barbershop and other community-based sites of connection and support be both helpful and not enough to address the mental health needs of our boys of color?

5 Which of the mental health support implementation practices identified below do you connect with the most.

| Make it Collective |

| Walk & Talk |

| Relevancy/Rapport |

| Culture & Identity |

| Explain it to them |

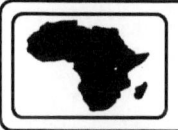

Dr. Malik Muhammad

5

Building Relationships and Repairing Harm: Restorative Practices

> " The teachers couldn't reach me
> and my mama couldn't beat me
> hard enough to match the pain of my Pop not seeing me.
> So, with that disdain in my membrane
> got on my pimp game.
> Fuck the world my defense became.
>
> Jay Z in "December 4th"

Whether in single gender or co-ed environments, we must organize our classrooms, schools, and organizations to connect, value authentic voice, honor cultural differences, and use our authority for the optimal development of the black and brown male personality. Restorative Practices play a significant role in this process. In my book *The Restorative Journey: The Theory and Application of Restorative Practices,* I provide a comprehensive introduction to Restorative Practices. In this chapter, I'll briefly introduce the framework and make explicit connection to what it means for our black and brown boys.

Emerging from the restorative justice movement, Restorative Practices establishes a progressive discipline framework to involve students in the school community. According to the International Institute for Restorative Practices (IIRP), "the fundamental hypothesis of restorative practices is that human beings are happier, more cooperative and productive, and more likely to make positive changes in their behavior when those in positions of authority do things *with* them, rather than to them or for them" and that the aim of restorative practices in school communities is to develop community and to manage conflict and tensions by repairing harm with an emphasis on restoring relationships. In our work in Akoben, we teach that Restorative Practices constitute seven practices ranging on a continuum from informal to formal:

- Affective Statements (proactive and responsive)
- Restorative Questions (responsive)
- Pulse Checks (proactive)
- Restorative Conversations (responsive)
- Responsive Circles (responsive)
- Proactive Circles (proactive)
- Formal Conferences (responsive)

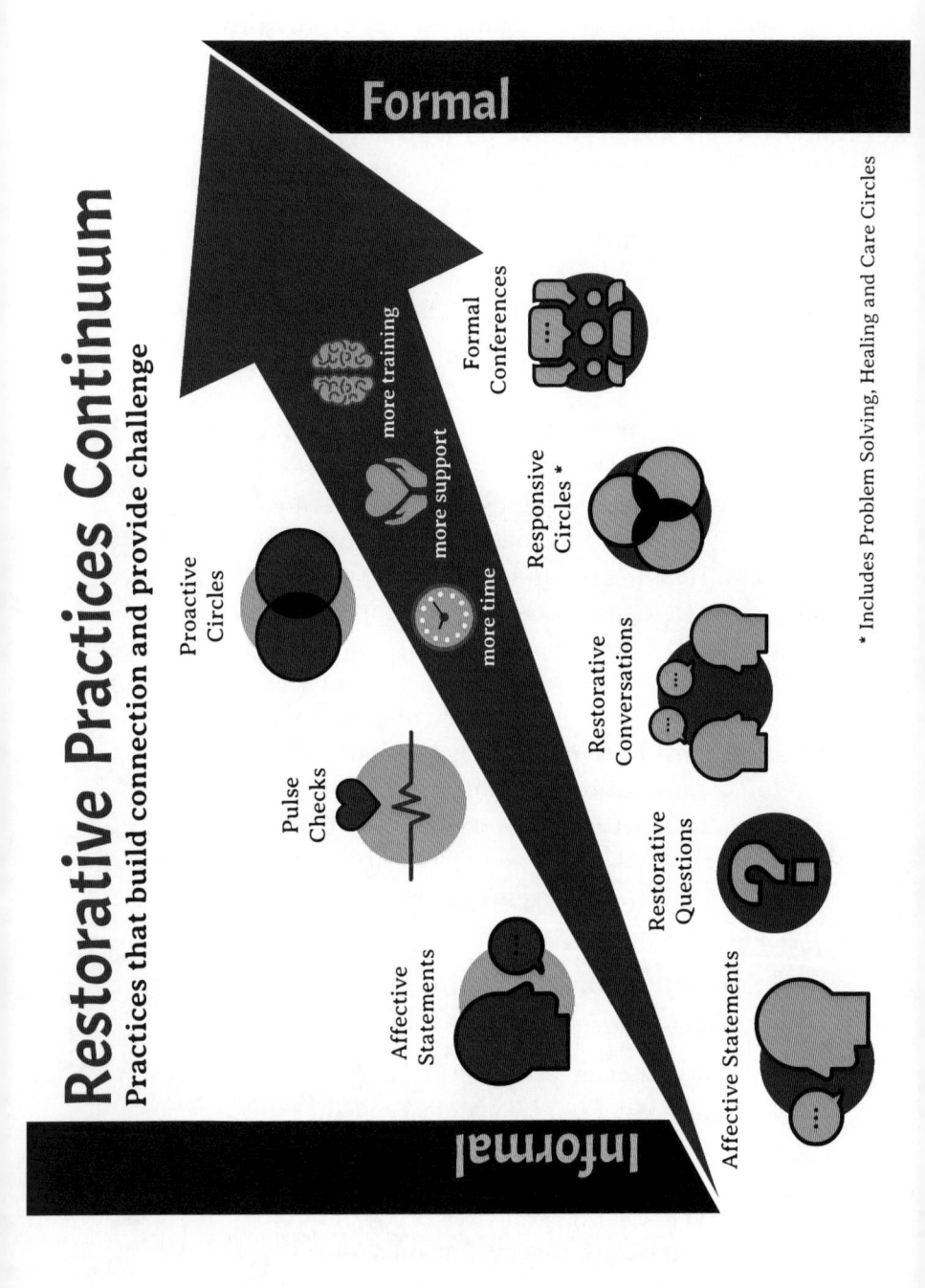

Restorative Practices Continuum

Practices that build connection and provide challenge

Informal → Formal

- Affective Statements
- Pulse Checks
- Proactive Circles
- Responsive Circles *
- Formal Conferences

- Affective Statements
- Restorative Questions
- Restorative Conversations

more time → more support → more training

* Includes Problem Solving, Healing and Care Circles

112 We Can Save Our Boys of Color

The illustration on the next page provides a way to understand this continuum of practices and is used within our core restorative practices training. Additionally, in The *Restorative Journey,* I explain each of these in detail and with practical application.

Research has shown that relational, prevention-based work coupled with responsive practices work. Schools, globally, report that serious harm and violent incidences decrease when they use restorative practices to work "with" students instead of the common punitive-centered paradigm (Lewis, 2009; Shaw, 2007).

The use of authority is central in our collective analysis and self-reflection on how we serve this population in a way that builds social capital on the one hand and effectively responds to wrongdoing on the other. Through our work in serving black and brown boys in public, charter and alternative schools, we find that Restorative Practices provide one of the most effective frameworks to analyze and shift our authority to build relationships and repair harm.

This fundamental and radical shift away from punishment-centered approaches is critical to save the lives of our boys of color and transform our use of authority in schools, law enforcement, service agencies, families, and the community. As was mentioned in Chapter 1, the outcomes for our Black and Latino boys indicate that they often do not feel connected to, valued by, or uplifted by many public institutions, including schools. They often find support and relationships among their peers, outside of the influence of adults who wield authority and bias toward them. The cycle of punishment-disconnectedness-negative behavior-punishment replicates itself throughout the school/life tenure of many black boys.

> "The excessive use of force creates legitimacy problems, and force without legitimacy leads to defiance, not submission."

Malcolm Gladwell in **David and Goliath**

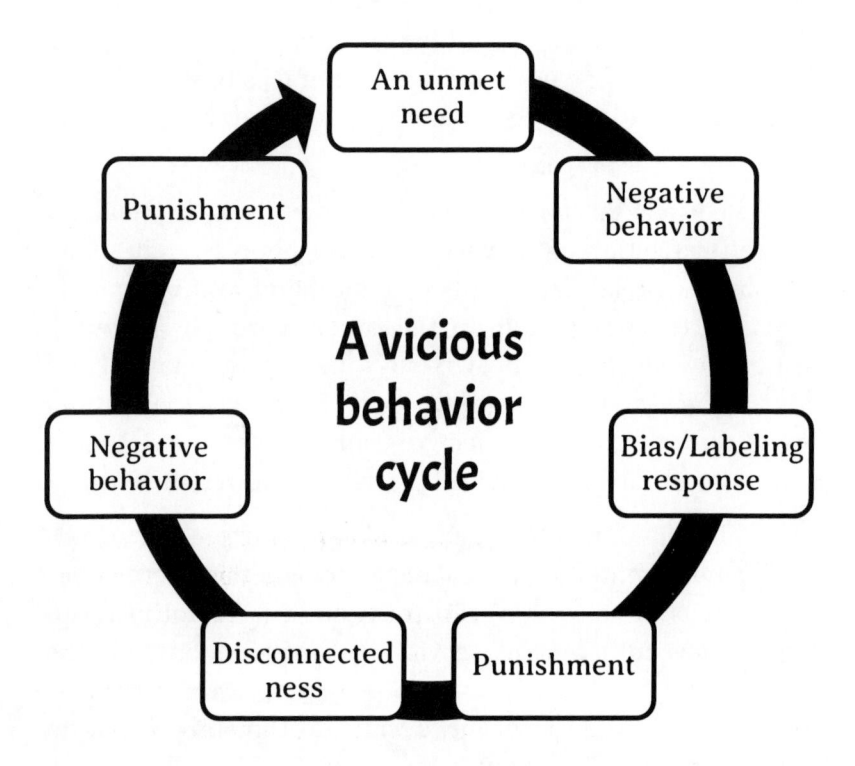

A vicious behavior cycle

- An unmet need
- Negative behavior
- Bias/Labeling response
- Punishment
- Disconnectedness
- Negative behavior
- Punishment

The Akoben Social Discipline Window

One of the most powerful frameworks that we use in Restorative Practices is the Social Discipline Window. This simple 2 x 2 matrix provides a tool of analysis that can flow from the superficial to the profound in understanding our use of authority. The Akoben Social Discipline Window[17] is unquestionably the most important element of our training material as well as my personal favorite piece to teach.

> **We can understand authority as being at the intersection of both connection and challenge.**

In the simplest of terms, we can understand authority as being at the intersection of both connection and challenge. By connection we refer to being nurturing, compassionate, wielding empathy, understanding, and love. The connection continuum, as represented on the Social Discipline Window as the horizontal line, ranges from high to low connection. By challenge we are referring to setting limits, establishing expectations, providing structure, pushing for results, holding folks accountable, and providing norms and standards. The challenge continuum, as represented on the Social Discipline Window as the vertical line, also ranges from high to low challenge. The quadrants thus created reflect the intersection and degree of connection and challenge in our usage of authority.

---

[17] The Akoben Social Discipline Window is an evolution and adaptation of the original one developed and popularized by the International Institute for Restorative Practices.

The Akoben Social Discipline Window

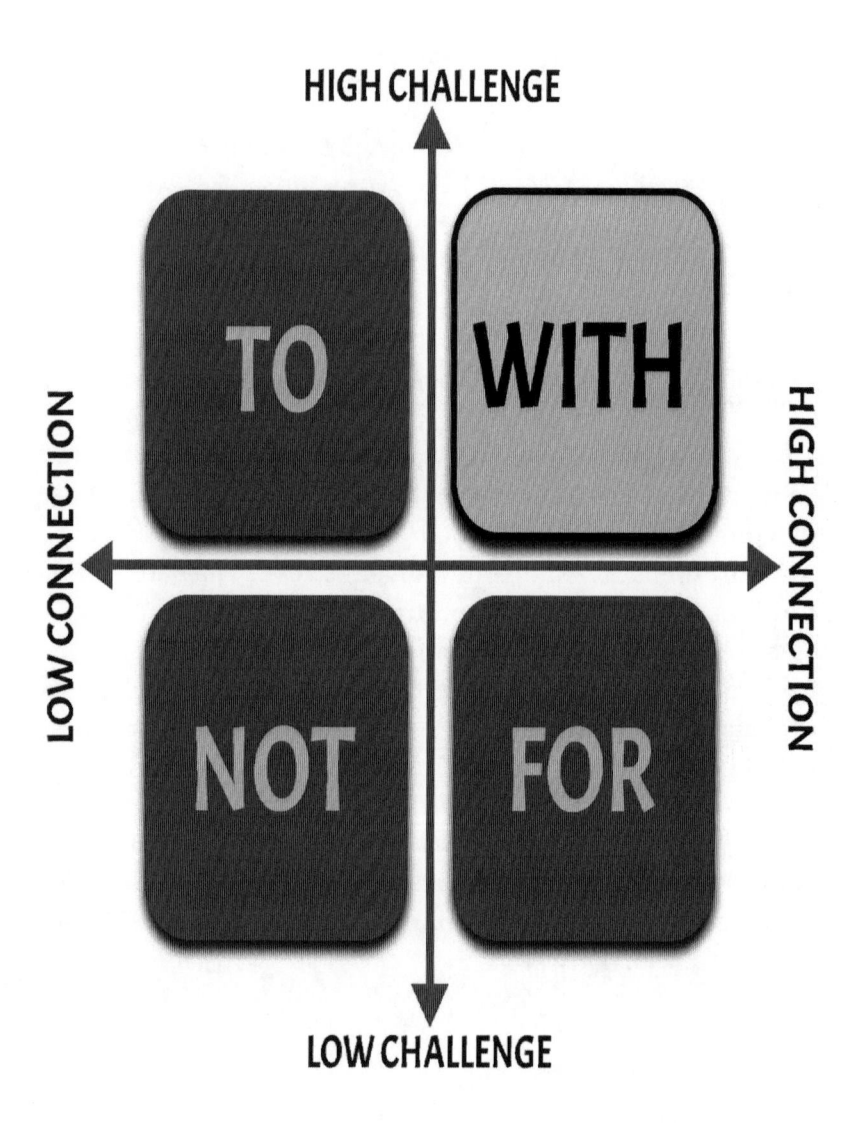

HIGH CHALLENGE

LOW CONNECTION | **HIGH CONNECTION**

TO	WITH
NOT	FOR

LOW CHALLENGE

The Not Box

The Not Box reflects the use of authority that is both low in connection and low in challenge. The teacher, administrator, Dean, parent, police officer, and/or community worker who operates in this box has made a choice to abdicate their responsibility, setting little to no limits and expressiong little to no compassion for our black and Latino boys. In their presence, our boys of color are given expressed permission to act-in or act-out without the adult correcting behavior, providing guidance/direction, and/or intervening with appropriate strength and seriousness. Additionally, our boys are clear that this adult disengagement is not centered in love or compassion; instead, it reflects the natural distancing created when faced with things you ignore. Therefore, we refer to this as the NOT box. The adults who operate from this space are NOT engaged, NOT effective, and truly NOT really there.

The TO Box

The TO Box represents the use of authority that is low in connection and high in challenge. We know this quadrant well as that of the authoritarian, dictator, heavy handed administrator, in short, the Joe Clark from Lean *on Me*. Sayings like "it's my way or the highway," "these kids have to learn the hard way... we can't baby them," "I'm not here to like you, I'm here to teach/lead/police you." While often disguised in the language of self-determination, and justified as a means to provide much needed-structure and prepare our boys of color for a challenging world, this use of authority finds value only in punitive forms of accountability—complaince and obedience. There is little interest in emotional intelligence or developing an internal locus of control within those they serve. On face value, there can be gains made and the needle moves on the metrics the adult finds most valuable (ie. Law and order, tests, safety). However, the gains are often short-lived and only an inch-deep because it weakens intrinsic motivation and creates a dependency upon the dominant adult rather than an authentic relationship of respect and bidirectional value. We refer to this quadrant as the TO box. The adults who operate from 'TO' approach use their authority to do things TO those they serve; or who serve them in this case.

The FOR Box

The polar opposite of the TO box, the FOR box represents high connection and low challenge. Here resides the leader, teacher, and/or community worker who acts from the heart and cherishes friendships with those they serve, but also operates from a deficiency mindset cloaked in praise and hugs. Excuses, struggles, and disabilities are all accepted and cited by them to underscore why they (and the rest of us) should carry much of the weight and not hold our boys of color accountable. Like their TO counterparts, the needle on some metrics can move, however we see a normalization of negative behavior and frustration once the pizza, immediate attention or other external rewards run out. We refer to this quadrant as the FOR box. The adults that are operating here use their authority to do things FOR those they serve.

The WITH Box

The WITH box is the opposite of the NOT box. It is the quadrant of full engagement through a blend of high connection and high challenge. Here, the adult sets clear limits and provides direction, holds young people accountable while nurturing their authentic personalities, respects their voice and needs, and builds strong connections. Effective, restorative leaders, educators, parents, and adults operate from this space with conscious effort and ongoing practice.

Through conscious effort we learn to operate from the WITH box because none of us are naturally in this quadrant. It takes work and effort to build our skills and comfort level to be here. When we think of the most positive adults who were in our own young lives, they most likely exemplified this balance between connection and challenge. Their high connection was rooted in unconditional love and their high challenge was rooted in the highest of expectations in believing in our potential. The adults who operate here engage, collaborate and do things WITH those they serve.

Our use of authority is influenced by a number of factors, including our backgrounds, emotional scripting around the need for power, control, acceptance, level of stress and coping capacity. Most of us fluctuate in our use of authority between the TO and FOR boxes. In reality, how we use our authority often has very little to do with meeting the needs of those we serve and more to do with what is going on with us personally. However, our decision to operate from the TO, FOR, NOT and WITH boxes always has an effect on the youth we serve, our colleagues, and it ripples out to impact families and the community. Let's understand now how the Social Discipline window uniquely impacts our black and Latino boys.

The Social Discipline Window and our Boys of Color

Although we laid out the challenges and deleterious effects of the school environment for our boys of color in Chapter One, we can now apply the Social Discipline Window framework to analyze the impact our use of authority has on our black and latino boys.

The NOT Box: You Don't Matter And Are Not Worthy

In over the nearly 500 Restorative Practices trainings I've facilitated across the world, I have never had a participant admit that they primarily operate in the NOT box. While some may, the twin pressures of shame and self-preservation keep most of us from admitting it. However, in visiting schools and organizations and in talking to many black and Latino boys themselves, we see and they describe many environments that certainly fall within this quadrant. For our boys of color (and other students), adults operating from the NOT box are the ones that they describe as not caring about them at all. The depersonalization and non-engagement that they receive in relationships with adults operating from the NOT box communicate a clear message for these boys—they don't matter. In fact, to hold a place of authority and potential adult influence in the lives of our most marginalized youth, and then not "see" them or ignore their behavior and need for connection and support is equal to, if not worse than, passive forms of violence against them. I believe that this is rooted in a belief that these boys are not worthy of our attention or best efforts. That serving *these* youth is where I have to be, not where I want to be.

The TO Box: You Must Be Controlled

Whereas, the NOT box ignores the value and needs of our boys of color, the TO and FOR boxes see them from lenses clouded by our own bias. The TO box operates from the dominant societal mindset that our Black and Latino boys must be controlled. Their very nature requires a heavy-hand, a dominant authoritarian figure whose primary role is to ensure obedience. The paradigm however is crafted and communicated under the guise of more structure and order. For instance, Dr. Ben Chavis, in his book <u>Crazy Like a Fox</u> (which does include some thoughtful insight from a passionate educator), champions the TO mentality when he states "when you look at the areas in which minorities succeed – sports, military, and church- you realize what they have in common...they are all highly structured and have serious consequences for stepping out of line (Chavis, 2009)." But the TO box encompasses three fundamental and significant errors. **First,** it is the replication and validation of the oppressive and violent tactics used on Black and Latino men for centuries. Plantations always used the strategy of control, dominance, and soul-breaking in the absence of support. We know that prisons continue to use the same strategies. In *The Classroom and the Cell,* Dr. Marc Lamont Hill, in conversation with Mumia Abu-Jamal, spoke about "the fact that prisons have become so normalized in our imaginations...which speaks to just how powerful the political and ideological machinery of the State has been (Abu-Jamal & Lamont Hill, 2011)." Intimidation threats, punishments, and hierarchies characterize these interactions. We know them well as the tools America used towards people of color historically and contemporarily to keep them in line and in their place. What is even more heartbreaking is that our boys begin to replicate this approach towards themselves, their peers, and others. **Secondly,** the TO approach induces and activates trauma. What I'm saying is that the TO approach often creates the event which can originate or exacerbate trauma, thereby creating a trauma-reaction. It induces the survival mechanism which produces hypermasculinity (fight), disengagement (flight) or

The TO box induces the survival mechanism which produces hypermasculinity (fight), disengagement (flight) or passivity (freeze) as coping mechanisms. In any case, learning stops for our boys of color.

Dr. Malik Muhammad

passivity (freeze) as coping mechanisms. In any case, learning stops for our boys of color. Additionally, it reinforces and emboldens the hypermasculinity that lives within the TO box approach already. **Lastly,** disproportionality in discipline finds its genesis in this quadrant. If our boys of color are more inclined to be controlled by teachers and administrators, then disproportionately punishing, suspending, and expelling them are natural and inevitable outcomes.

The FOR Box: You Are Deficient And Need Me To Save You

Perhaps more subtle, but no less damaging to our boys of color is the FOR box. When adults behave with only support and refuse to establish norms and accountability, they are fortifying and promoting a deficiency mindset. You are effectively saying: *I won't set high standards, or any standards at all, because they are incapable of meeting them. I won't push them and apply pressure because the answers lie in me (to do it for them) and not them. They are deserving only of my praise and rewards, not challenge and correction.*

This lack of faith in and expectation from our boys of color combined with the heavy dose of savior syndrome produces a set of negative mental habits for them. Dependency is the most natural outcome.

> **Accolades preceding effort is self-defeating and dependency creating.**
> -*Mwalimu Bomani Baruti*

When our boys are not required to carry the weight of their own education or family and social responsibilities, then literally and figuratively their naturally strong shoulders become atrophied. They grow accustomed to teachers giving the answers to the hardest problems if they just wait it out. They grow comfortable with community workers giving them a pass when arriving late to programs. They come to expect that their parents will accept (and even provide) their excuses for why they behaved in a negative way. Mwalimu Bomani Baruti in his book *Asafo* is correct when he states:

> "By running interference for our sons when the tasks are hard and challenging and within their capacity, we are weakening them for their life's responsibilities, therefore, making them 1) unprepared, 2) dependent and soft, and 3) ripe for the whim of anyone who will feed them (Baruti, 2015)."

A problematic mindset develops as an outcome of this dependency. If we have treated them as though they should be coddled and pitied, they learn that they should and can get us to do their work—school work, life-work,--for them. Our own cajoling and coercing them into behaving (or at least liking us) teaches them that these are acceptable methods to use authority and manage behavior. What happens when they direct this quid pro quo attitude at young women or girls? What happens when they attempt to cajole her by doing something FOR her (providing a gift or compliment) and she doesn't respond as intended? What happens when their well-used explanation about tough family conditions don't land the same on their college professor or supervisor. What happens when their son's daiper needs to be changed and they have never had to do it themselves. Too often, we see this lead to emotional or physical retaliation.

In many situations across education, employment and family, too many of our boys of color, steeped heavily within a FOR approach, have learned to ask for rather than do for himself.

Lastly, the FOR quadrant cripples intrinsic motivation and drive to struggle through challenges. It weakens the fighting capacity and sense of meritorious achievement. It is cute to encourage our Black and Latino boys that they

> **Without the internal fortitude to accept both help and responsibility, then they will rise no further than our low expectations of them.**

can become anything, but if we don't allow them to carry the weight, then what will they become? Without the internal fortitude to accept both help and responsibility, then they will rise no further than our low expectations of them. In *The Fire Next Time,* Baldwin so eloquently explains this limiting mindset for boys and men of color:

> "The limits of your ambition were, thus, expected to be set forever. You were born into a society which spelled out in brutal clarity, and in as many ways as possible, that you were a worthless human being. You were not expected to aspire to excellence; you were expected to make peace with mediocrity (Baldwin, 1992)."

Two Paradigms

In Chapters One and Two, we explained the challenges for our boys of color (and we who serve them) in our current school contexts. With few exceptions, the status quo can largely be understood as a Punitive Paradigm. That is, school environments focus on punitive consequences to maladaptive behavior and the implementation of expedient standard techniques which often break relationships instead of developing them. There is an emphasis on naming, identifying, and determining who committed the infraction or crime. We spend a great deal of energy and paper on documenting the infraction in detail. We have paragraphs in the code of conduct defining "class disturbance" vs "interrupting the learning process" and "fighting" vs "bullying." Within the punitive model, naming the rule broken or crime done is extremely important. Once we believe that we've named it properly, we then devote the remainder of our energy on determining the severity of the sanction or consequence. Should the offender get a parent phone call, detention for 30 minutes or 45 minutes, or should they get a 1, 2, 3 or 10-day suspension? Should it be in-school or out-of-school suspension? And, what does our Code of Conduct say anyway? The major advantage of this model is that it is expedient and fairly simple. In fact, it is so simple at times that we don't need to apply much thinking or discernment, just merely implement the code as someone else designed it. The greatest disadvantage, and harm, is that it doesn't give much, if any thought to the harm caused by the infraction.

Punitive Model
"Power-Based"

Infraction/Crime

causes

HARM

REQUIRES

Severity of Sanction

Restorative Model
"Collective-Based"

Infraction/Crime

causes

HARM

creates

NEEDS

REQUIRES

Repair and Restoration

Also, it assumes that the sanction/consequence will both curb or change the behavior of the one who caused harm and satisfy the needs of those harmed. Too often, neither is true.

For our boys of color and all students, Restorative Practices provides the opportunity to create school and community environments that respond differently to wrongdoing. In the Restorative Model, the wrongdoing is identified, but much more attention is given to who was harmed/affected and in what way. This is an inclusive perspective, looking at the intended victim *and* to others affected as well. Likewise, we explore and attempt to understand what needs were created by this harm.

For instance, a teacher who was pushed down by two student's fighting in the hallway might have the real need for physical therapy as well as having his sense of safety restored, while the offender may have the real need to apologize, express their remorse, or be removed from others for a time period. Lastly, a great emphasis is placed on what actions the wrongdoer and community must do to repair and restore relationships, balance and peace. These "consequences" are directly linked to addressing the needs created by the harm of the infraction/crime.

Relationships As the Decisive Factor

In our experience we have found that the most significant and decisive factor in effective disciplinary consequences for lasting and transformative change is the quality of the relationship between the student and adult. In short, when it comes to discipline, relationships are the decisive factor. In the absence of a relationship, we are, at best, guessing at what will have a meaningful impact on the student to transform their behavior. What happens when our suspensions don't work on Anthony because we just rewarded him with a three-day vacation from school, where he would rather not be anyway? What happens when our reward of cute little fuzzy pencils doesn't induce Jamal to return the failed test signed by a parent? How are we going to handle Javier when he could care less about not being allowed to go on the upcoming field trip to the museum? It is inside of a relationship with these guys that we would accomplish at least two things. First, we begin to understand what their leverage points are. That is, what has meaning to them. More importantly (and less manipulative perhaps), through this relationship, they establish a sense of belonging and connection with us, which makes actions that threaten to disappoint, harm or lose the relationship much more significant. Ultimately, if we really want our consequences to have an effect beyond simple punishment, then we must connect the student to our school community through relationships.

Additionally, relationships are a determining factor for academic achievement as well. According to Hattie (2008),

> *"A classroom's social glue is not just an extra enhancement; it has real academic significance. With a strong 0.72 effect size, student-teacher relationships are in the top 10 of all student achievement factors, and group cohesion and peer influences have a strong 0.53 effect size. Contrast these with the surprisingly low 0.09 effect size for teacher content knowledge* (Hattie, 2008)"

Too, support and connection are critical in developing trauma-supportive and responsive environments. "For example, social bonding and trust help mitigate the adverse effects of chronic stress by prompting the brain to release oxytocin, a neuropeptide that suppresses the "classic" stress hormones, such as cortisol (Kosfeld, Heinrichs, Zak, Fischbacher, & Fehr, 2005; Leuner & Shors, 2013)." In other words, just like we are hurt in relationships, it is relationships that help us to heal.

But how do we Build Relationships?

The process for building positive relationships with youth, especially our boys of color, is an illusive one. The incubator for developing these relationship—not only between the adult and young person, but between them themselves—are environments that build social capital. We define social capital as the degree of connections among people in a particular community which enable it to function positively and effectively. Here are some key steps to build social capital:

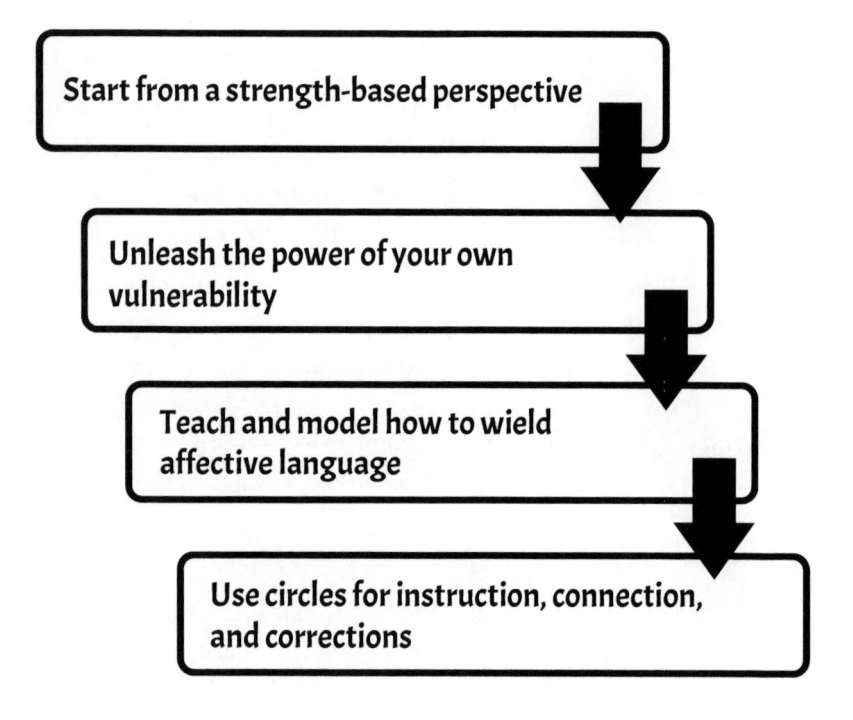

- Start from a strength-based perspective
- Unleash the power of your own vulnerability
- Teach and model how to wield affective language
- Use circles for instruction, connection, and corrections

The last two steps, affective language and circles, are deeply embedded in our work around Restorative Practices and Trauma Informed Care. These have powerful ramifications for our specialized work with boys of color. Let's take time to explore these two practices now.

Wielding Affective Language

Again we refer to the brilliance of Dr. Christina Watlington when she states that "in the absence of a strong emotional vocabulary, we all rely on our behavioral vocabulary." In the absence of access to language which expresses affect, emotion and feelings, all of us will communicate what is going on with us through the expression of our behavioral vocabulary. If a student doesn't feel safe or is not skilled enough to raise his hand and express frustration and confusion, then he will show us through nonverbal behavior which could range from a dazed look of mental detachment to aggressive backlash against the teacher or other students. Similarly, if the Assistant Principal doesn't have the words to express her burnout and feelings of being overwhelmed, her behavioral vocabulary might kick in by avoidance of work or disrespect towards her colleagues. If we can understand that this is a universal phenomenon that affects us all, it might allow for us to have more patience and recognize the humanity in our youth when they struggle.

Now, what happens when a student doesn't just struggle to verbally express emotion but it is socially unacceptable and, in some cases, dangerous to express certain emotions? What happens when the pressure to deny all but a few emotions is intimately wrapped up in the core of your self-identity? Or when social stereotypes and unconsious biases against black and brown boys limits their emotional range. When anger, pride and happiness are the full range of your emotional continuum, and they become the filter through which you manifest shame, humiliation, sadness and fear. Such is the case with many boys and men in general, but specifically with our boys [and men] of color, who represent in the Western psyche, the quintessential male other. The culture of masculinity and hypermasculinity prevents them/us from expressing what George M. Taylor refers to as "our inner lives and truths."

I refer to the ability to express the full range of emotion verbally as "wielding affective language." That is, the ability of our boys to communicate verbally when they are sad, frustrated, overjoyed, ashamed, and fascinated, etc. Just like the development and understanding of any language, this is taught, encouraged and refined by adults who care about the youth they serve. We teach affective language through both modeling and explicit instruction.

When we make affective statements ourselves or ask affective questions of our youth, we are engaging in the process of modeling and teaching affective language. Here are examples of affective statements:

> "Malik, I am excited because you came to the center today prepared with your tutoring materials and a positive attitude."

> "Alex, when you were cursing in front of the elderly women on the field trip, I felt (and still feel) embarassed and frustrated."

> "I'm confused and angry right now Javier because you promised us that you would be here at noon and your late again."

Notice that they all include 3 critical elements:

- All are "I" statements. They communicate what is going on with the speaker, expressing only their understanding and perspective.

- All communicate emotion. Whether that emotion is excitement, embarrassment, frustration, confusion, or anger, each statement includes the expression of the emotion of the speaker.

- All identify behavior. The speaker highlights the behavior which elicited their emotion so that the listener can understand the impact of their actions.

Another example of this is described by Eric Jensen:

> "Listen, you're a good kid. Earlier, I was expecting you to show [appropriate emotion], and you didn't. Most adults will expect *this* [show the desired response]. I know that's not what you would normally do, but adults expect it, and I want you to stay out of trouble. Let me show you what I was looking and listening for (Jensen, 2013)."

When adults use affective statements, they are not only modeling emotional language but also helping our boys of color (and others too) understand how their behavior affects others. This is a profoundly important process of building empathy. The greatest challenge here is that it requires a willingness to be vulnerable.

Being emotionally vulnerable when appropriate not only models this for our boys of color but also communicates to them that they are someone worthy of your attention, care, and concern. You demonstrate, better than anything else, that there is a connection and relationship between the two of you. I argue that we develop and build these connections even more by reaching out to them first, being human with them first, being vulnerable with them first. This means that we have to shoot down all idiotic advice like "don't smile until January" because this doesn't lead to authentic connection. We reach to them first and consistently and then look for and recognize it when they reach back to us.

> **We reach to them first and consistently, and then look for and recognize it when they reach back to us.**

The Circle: A Powerful and Indigenous Process

There is no single structure more characteristic of Restorative Practices than the Circle. Many superb books have been written on the power and effectiveness of the circle process[18]. Here, I'd like to highlight the particular value of the circle for boys of color as well as analyze an indigenous circle process not fully understood by many, including some of its own practitioners.

In our experience, the circle's greatest value is its ability to foster authentic connection between participants. Authentic connection where our black and Latino boys and the adults who support them get an opportunity to have voice and bond, where we get to see the humanity in each other, thus making it much harder to hurt and choose to violate each other. Authentic connection where moral authority and empathy rule over titles, age, or other categories that create us and the "other." Circle practice reaches a level of youth participation far beyond hearing a student's voice over the loudspeaker during the morning announcements or reciting the pledge of allegiance. It's more than simply asking students which book they want to read during quiet reading time, and it is so much deeper than asking for parent chaperones to attend a class trip to the local amusement park. We are talking about facing each other throughout the day to listen and share in the collective understanding of our school tribe.

According to Boyes-Watson, the Circle is also powerful because it doesn't include the traditional symbols of power and significance: No table to hide behind, no podium for power, no back of the room, no symbols of hierarchy. This

---

[18]Some of my favorite include Dr. Carolyn Boyes-Watson's *Peacemaking Circles and Urban Youth* and Dr. Maureen Fitzgerald's *Corporate Circles*. Of course, there is also *The Restorative Journey: The Theory and Application of Restorative Practices*.

is precisely what speaks most to youth who, by definition, are without power or position, therefore voice (Boyes-Watson, 2008).

In Chapter Two we critiqued the culturally imperialistic approaches to certain school interventions with our boys of color. If we are not careful, the circle could be approached in a similar way, as something that we are bringing to these boys to help them. On a restorative level, we should invite them to sit in our circle, but more importantly,

> **" There is a very big difference between being told you are equal and feeling and seeing that you are equal. The Circle looks and feels like a place of genuine equality.**
> - Molly Baldwin

find ways to join theirs. Of course, this means that we have to understand them and they, us. When we genuinely begin to understand them, we find that there exists within the culture of many urban (or urban-oriented) Black and Latino boys an indigenous circle process. It is called the Cipher.

The Cipher as a Powerful Restorative Practice

Imagine a spontaneous circle formed by seven middle school boys of color immediately after school in the courtyard. Their bodies are huddled tight and there is an intensity of energy among the boys. Voices grow louder and other students flock toward the group. As the closest adult, you intervene and elbow your way toward the center since your voice and shouts don't seem to have any effect. Bodies are swaying closer to the epicenter and some hands are in the air. The "ooh," "damn" and "whaat" coming from the crowd tell you that an afterschool fight is happening. You know these kids and didn't hear about anyone having beef with anyone

Dr. Malik Muhammad

today. When you finally get into the center, you bump into Ali, a physically underdeveloped rambunctious 6th grader who is shouting something to the inner circle. Now at the center of the circle, you look around to see who Ali was fighting and you only see him and everyone else looking back at you with angry eyes. Unbeknownst to you, you just interrupted one of the strongest lyricists in the school as he was just 24 seconds into his freestyle flow. When you scan the inner circle, two more of the boys have their hands to their mouths delivering the bass and rhythm beats for Ali while another one has his phone out live streaming the whole process. Beyond them are twenty more fully engaged youth, who normally fall asleep during your math class and never have questions when you bring in a guest speaker or ever join school clubs. There was no fighting, no crisis, just connection. You just broke up a cipher.

The cipher is a uniquely indigenous phenomenon, adapted to the modern context by urban youth as a dynamic way to express themselves. Its modern manifestation is as an outlet for various expressions of hip-hop culture, including mc'ing (rap lyrical expression), beatboxing and b-boying (dancing). Additionally, several conscious groups like the Five Percenter Nation of Gods and Earths would use the cipher to "build" (share knowledge and co-create culture) with each other. The cipher is a site for sharing, for free and authentic expression, for connection, and for "battle." It is a street-based cyclical exchange of energy. It is a sacred space that one does not enter into lightly, but has its own set of norms and structure, including:

- Only one person has the floor at a time
- One must be invited/embraced by the collective
- Everyone contributes, no matter how small
- Challenging another is acceptable
- Contributions determine length
- Authentic and freestyle participation
- Flow with the rhythm of the collective
- We celebrate each other

The most sacrosanct of the cipher's norms is authentic expression. One must only come from the "top of the dome" or "from your heart" or your contribution will be questioned and collectively and publicly lamb basted. This shaming can be reintegrative as the person who violates this cardinal rule might remain within the cipher and possibly given another chance to now share their authentic voice/contribution.

Authenticity and sincere voices rarely conform to the acceptable and stale methods of expression and decibel levels of traditional school. Therefore, ciphers almost always find home within the wild and open free time of youth (ie. Street corners, parks, afterschool, etc). Additionally, ciphers create and build on energy. As we explored in Chapters One and Two, we have come to outlaw and criminalize the energy of our boys of color within the context of school. The cipher can be unpredictable and dynamic, two traits that traditional and oppressive environments can not and will not tolerate with black and Latino boys.

The type of connection made through the use of a circle goes deep into the historical memory of our boys of color. We leaned into the circle to sustain life and humanity, even in our darkest times of enslavement:

> *"We gathered and enjoyed the warmth of our commonness, of our togetherness. We would form a circle, each touching those next to us so as to physically express our spiritual closeness. We 'testified,' speaking on the day's or week's experiences. We share the pain of those experiences and received from the group affirmations of our existence as suffering beings. As we "lay down our burdens," we became lighter. As we testified and listened to others testify, we begin to understand ourselves as communal beings, no longer the "individual" that the slave system tried to make us... Through our participation in these rituals, we became one. We became, again, a community. Each of us gained the strength necessary to deal with our incarceration. Sometimes we prepared for rebellion* (Ani, 1994).*"*

Further evidence of this lies in the Adinkra symbols of the Akan, used as powerful philosophical references to the spirit of African people. The oldest and chief of these ancient symbols is the Adinkrahene which is a set of concentric circles. It is believed to be the origin of all other symbols and represents leadership, greatness, and charisma. When we tap into the power of the circle, we are validating and empowering a natural method of interaction for our boys (and girls and ourselves).

Baba Kwame Agyei Akoto was an amazing elder and profound voice in the African Centered school movement, and one of the founders of NationHouse and Watoto Shule in Washington, DC. He argued that circles are the preferred and most culturally sound methodology of instruction between the mwalimu (teacher) and mwanafunzi (student). In his seminal work, *Nationbuilding,* he explained that their interaction should be "interactive, meaning that there is a vibrant exchange of information, mutual learning and inspiration" and that "this interactive and reciprocal act of communication...is exemplified by the communal circle in traditional Afrikan societies. According to Baba Agyei (Akoto, 1992) the circle:

- facilitates the spiritual communion in traditional spiritual systems.

- includes the family elder or griot and represents the intergenerational flow of history and culture.

- is explicitly collective and communal and can best facilitate the kind of dynamic and reciprocal discourse that is essential to the development of the truly liberated Afrikan personality.

- is particularly well-suited to facilitate the active participation of all its members, and it allows the mwalimu to easily adjust from an egalitarian posture to that of mediator, facilitator, lecturer, adversary, and various degrees in between.

- is fluid enough that opportunity for mwanafunzi initiative and creativity is possible.

- it can further the development of cooperative skills and a sense of reciprocity and mutual accountability.

- it can also facilitate the development of leadership and constituent skills.

For our boys of color, the use of the circle goes beyond the simple implementation of a restorative program, but also has the power to tap into both their indigenous and culturally normative mode of exchange as well as the modern expression of such in the Cipher.

A Challenge to Restorative Practitioners

We owe a great debt and appreciation to our colleagues within the Restorative Practices movement for championing and broadening the use of these powerful practices, including affective statements and circles, within schools and beyond. We have learned from, struggled alongside, and immersed ourselves in this good work with them for many years now.

As we imagine the next evolution of this work, it must consciously and explicitly address the challenges facing our black and Latino boys and men, the most marginalized among us. This will require us to overtly confront issues of power, oppression, racism, sexism, white privilege, male privilege, and heterosexual privilege. Teaching restorative skills without leading our training participants to challenge their own biases does not go nearly far enough. In other words, the challenge is to sharpen our restorative practices as tools of equity and liberation, rather than simply dulling the negative effects of oppression.

The Practical Application and Challenges to Implementation

I have had the honor of learning from and with one of the most preeminent practitioners of Restorative Practices in the world, Mr. Steve Korr. We work closely in leadership at Akoben and have spent many hours discussing restorative practices as a critical approach to serving our black and

Latino boys. In a recent conversation with Steve, we focused on several elements of practical application and challenges. Here are recommendations for implementation:

Build it WITH them, not FOR them:

At Akoben, we firmly believe that Restorative Practices does not belong to the adults in the community, but also to the youth. That is why we launched the **Akoben Student Champion Program** to build up the development and capacity of young people to implement these practices. As we teach them, we are learning with them innovative and thoughtful ways of doing this work of proactive community building and responsive repair to harm. To learn more about the Akoben Student Champion Program, visit www.akobenllc.org.

Point out the bias fiercely but with love:

A restorative approach gives us the process to confront biases with fierce love, utilizing connection and challenge. Steve talks about challenging folks in a delicate way. Sometimes saying "listen to the words of what you're saying." Or the reflective listening technique of just repeating it back to them, adding "Is this what you're saying? Is this what you truly believe?" Alot of the times when people get directly confronted about it and let it marinate a little bit, they see that no, its not their true belief but maybe is a manifestation of their frustration.

Find examples within the culture:

An important part of our work is to help people of color become conscious of our unconscious traditions. For instance, if we are a people that circle together, and we are, then this is not just white people stuff, this is our stuff. If we are a people that speak with emotional language then speaking emotionally is not just white people stuff, it's our stuff. This is about increasing the consciousness of our unconscious behavior on an internal and external level.

Resist the urge to replicate the harm of the world:

We should actively pushback against a common approach of replicating the harm our black and Latino boys receive from the world in a misguided attempt to prepare them for it. What we have heard often is "I am going to be really harsh because the world is harsh, right? They need to understand that the world is mean and nasty towards them." We must resist this reactionary, and ultimately shameful approach, which is particularly egregious because we'll spend all this time teaching them hardness and emotional separation and then blaming it on them down the road when they're not functioning the way we want to see.

Connection and Challenge is about relevancy:

There are culturally relevant ways, some healthy, that our black and Latino boys have in order to both connect and challenge each other. To the outsider or those lacking in cultural literacy, these interactions can be misunderstood if even seen at all. The slight head nod, the dap, the 'side-eye', and even the seemingly harsh cracking on/joking, can, at times, be understood as a healthy way of connecting or "checking" your brother. Of course, it is contextual, and we should use a curious lens to understand instead of judging initially.

Reflection & Application

1. Reflect on a recent challenging interaction you had with a boy of color. In which box did you fall in the Akoben Social Discipline Window? How did that work for you both?

2. How do the Two Paradigms help us understand the intersection of criminal justice and education and the school to prison pipeline?

3. Write at least 3 Affective statements that describe how you were feeling while reading this chapter.

4. Go online and check out a video of a cipher (sometimes spelled cypher). What are some of the norms and strengths that you notice? How might some of these be incorporated into your own facilitation of circles?

6

An Action Plan for Connectedness

> A whole bunch of gifts and a lot of presents It's not the presents, it's your presence and the essence of being there and showing him that you care.
>
> *Ed O.G. & Da Bulldogs*

Our criticism all along has been simple: schools and educational systems tasked with serving our most marginalized students, boys of color, too often perpetuate negative life trajectories that are killing them early. We offered three solutions thus far: single gender environments, mental health supports and restorative practices. Our recommendations in this book and subsequent books are centered on connectedness and relationships. While much of this work is rooted in restoration and healing, it is critical that we understand the proactive need for deeper connection and relationships. Limiting this work to being responsive at best or reactive at worst is an error. If we become trauma-informed, restorative, or culturally relevant solely to heal, respond to wrongdoing or address an issue, then we will perpetually chase after crises with our boys of color and others. An important value of this work is its ability to build peace and success by establishing a framework for connection and belonging. We are working to bond and connect people, including our black and Latino boys, to a community, sometimes after an incident or wrongdoing, but hopefully in lieu of one. We assert that all folks, those we serve as well as ourselves, can benefit from environments where we have voice, connection and are seen primarily through our strengths. This means that this work is not just to fix broken things, but to strengthen our bonds and relationships to prevent us from breaking them in the first place. Therefore, here are some additional key elements that can enliven an Action Plan for Connectedness in serving our Black and Latino boys:

> **❝ Despite our care for them, we do not welcome them into our midst, we service them. They become objects.**
>
> *- Peter Block*

1. **Begin with their story:**

    Boys of color have little opportunity to define the issues they are concerned about and determine how they want to deal with them. They are used to being lectured to and ignored. It is vital to start any work with these young men by asking them about their lives and their stories and creating room to talk about the kinds of relationships, families, communities, and institutions they would like to create and be a part of.

2. **Stay positive:**

    Many boys of color will assume they're going to be blamed for the issues they are facing, so they need to hear again and again that they have an important and valuable role to play in their community and relationships.

3. **Put trust and relationships at the center:**

    Boys of color, and young people in general, respond best to people they feel care about them. If part of our goal is to teach our boys about the importance of trust and respect in their relationships, it's vital that we model trust and respect in our relationships with young men.

4. **Meet them where they are:**

    In doing this work, we want our boys to grow in their awareness of important issues and in their willingness to engage in transformation and positive relationships. However, we can't let our vision of where we want them to go obscure our sense of where they are. It's important to let our boys teach us about where they are during our time with them. If they can't connect with the music, movies, sports figures, or actors we use as examples, we need to ask them to supply examples. It's important to avoid assuming that they are incapable of experiencing a wide range of emotions and to check in with them about what they're feeling. And it's important to consider that they experience masculinity in different ways, so it's valuable to think of and be sensitive to different masculinities present.

5. **Check your own assumptions:**

We can't afford to believe we are completely free of stereotypes, especially when middle schools, high schools, and colleges are rife with different social groups of young men: jocks, brains, preppies, queers, thugs, geeks, and so on. Be aware of whether our boys or young men from particular social groups seem to trigger strong emotions in you. Use your response as an opportunity to reach past social divisions and assumptions as well as to investigate your own reactions. Stay curious for the sake of your own growth and impact.

6. **Wait a little bit on the tough issues:**

Don't feel like you must deal with the hard topics right away. Give yourself time to build relationships with them before you tackle some of the issues you think they're going to struggle with most. Some examples of tough topics, depending on the group you're working with, are sexual violence, homophobia, and gender and class privilege. Most of the time it makes sense to start with low and medium risk questions/topics and then logically segue to more difficult topics.

7. **Seek leaders:**

Who are the boys of color other boys of color look up to? A young man who started his own business? Captain of the basketball team? Editor of the school newspaper? Consult with teachers, staff, and other youth-serving professionals to find out. Find ways to connect with these male student leaders. They can have a strong, positive impact on other young men. Also, let's also be on the lookout for those boys who have sway and influence, even if they currently don't have a leadership role, or better yet, haven't been acting in comfortable ways for adults. Let's not just privilege those boys of color who conform.

8. **Focus on stories:**

Don't you like to hear a good, personal story? So do our boys—especially stories that relate to masculinity and personal triumph. They live every day with the pressures and challenges of society, and if we share stories of our struggles and the struggles of men we have known, it opens the door for our boys to share their struggles. The telling of stories is essential if we are working to make boys of color more aware of both the dominant narratives of masculinity and the counter stories-those stories that exist in tension with prevailing notions of what it means to be a boy and man of color.

9. **Make action easy:**

Asking boys of color to challenge themselves in everyday situations involving the cultural attitudes supporting negative views of them is a most difficult challenge. It may take the most prolonged period of time to realize. So, help them along the action path. Assist them in developing structured personal interventions and create opportunities for them to practice positive responses often.

10. Be patient:

Change is hard for all of us. Frequently, it requires considerable testing of the waters. Initially, boys of color feel safest expressing their newly developing views of a positive, healthier self in the context of your meetings with them. And they will sometimes express a mix of attitudes and assumptions, some of which are tied to the very attitudes we want them to challenge. When we give our boys the space and support needed to develop a more secure sense of how they can choose to be stronger, healthier, and more resilient young men, they will become positive role models for other young men.

11. Have regular check-ins:

If you meet regularly with your boys of color, consider instituting a check-in at the beginning of every meeting. Check-ins are basically a go-around where each briefly shares where he's at, how he's feeling, what's going on in his life, how school's going, and so on. If important issues come up in the check-in, don't be too rigid about the planned agenda. Allow adequate space to discuss their issues.

12. Provide Incentives:

Most of us want something in return, and boys of color are no different. While it might be gratifying to assume that they will automatically see and embrace the long-term benefits of connecting with you, it doesn't hurt to pave the way with some short-term incentives. Bring food and snacks to share to meetings and ask them to do the same. Provide T-shirts for them. Give awards for the best growth of the year, and so on.

13. Provide male role models:

Our boys need to see as many positive adult role models as possible to feel supportive men surround them. Host a "Men of Strength" Day. Invite four or five men doing valuable work related to social justice and personal transformation to speak with a group of your boys to explain the ins and outs of their journey, why they have the values they do, and how they're making a difference. Aim for men of color who can connect in relevant ways with our boys of color.

14. Get involved in other ways:

Don't limit your interactions with boys of color to school or organizational meetings. Attend a sports event they're competing in. Take them to a movie and have a discussion afterward. Play video games together. Learn from them about ways you can be a part of their lives. Getting involved above and beyond workshops and meetings sends a clear message to them: **you matter to me.**

7

Closing Thoughts

As I mentioned in the Introduction, this book has been in the making for over a decade and pulls together some of the lessons I've been learning for the past 30 years. As I struggled with the project, I eventually consciously gave myself an "out" by breaking the book down into two volumes. To be honest, part of this was to give myself the freedom to have some breathing room, a half-time moment, if you will, to reflect and then fall back in love with the project. The other reason was to honor good learning theory, which requires us to study, learn, plan, practice, and repeat. It is true that power begins on the level of conception, but it is manifested through action. My hope is that the ideas presented here contribute to the ideological discussion, and just as importantly, the practices named come to life through concrete action in service of our black and Latino boys.

> **Power begins on the level of conception but is manifested through action.**
> - All-African People's Revolutionary Party

In this volume, we have worked through the case against the current deleterious conditions for our boys of color in schools, and for the case of supporting them intentionally and specifically. Here are a few critical take-aways that are important to me that you leave with:

- It doesn't take courage for us to focus on our boys of color, it just takes a belief in the practice of triage. Look at the data and go serve those who are struggling the most. Thats it, no courage needed.
- Accept that what we have been doing has not worked and that doing more of it won't save our boys of color, especially if those interventions are the universal, tier 1 supports that everyone gets.
- Constantly look for "wins" with our boys to build up confidence and the metacognitive muscle that helps them see and believe that they can succeed. This is going to mean that we might need to create the conditions at first to help them win, then increase the challenge from there.
- We all have a place in this fight to save our black and brown boys. If you are a white or female educator, and you find these boys struggling on your part of the battlefield, this work is yours. Continue to roll up your sleeves, implement the practices and simultaneously look for black and brown men to help support and guide the work with you.
- Spend time with our boys as often as possible, learn their language, hopes, concerns, and flow. What's more powerful than them coming into your circle is being invited into theirs. The only price for this is your evident trust, vulnerability, and love.
- Remember the righteousness of this work, especially when it's hardest to do. Be inspired and encouraged, we are making gains in many places with individuals and groups of boys. Take heart, you are on the right side of justice.

I believe, now more than ever, that we can really save our boys of color, not because the conditions have lessened, but because some of us are now better warriors at this work, more organized, and more determined than ever. I addressed my struggle with the notion of "saving" them from the outset in this book, but reaffirm that as we save them, we are teaching them the CPR and surviving to thriving skills, so they emerge as heroes in their own journey. This might just be the most important contribution I can make in my professional life. Let's do this together!

> **Somebody told me that a warrior never lets a warrior lack inspiration. We need you now!**
>
> *- Tubby Love in Lionheart*

Role Models & Resources[19]

I have included a traditional bibliography later in the book, but I wanted to give a special place to acknowledge the good work of several practitioners who are saving our boys of color. I have listed a few here, but recognize that I unfortunately will have missed many more. Please let me know about your work so that it can be mentioned in updated versions of this book:

Coalition of Schools Educating Boys of Color (COSEBOC)

It felt like home when I found COSEBOC and began attending and presenting at their annual Gathering. It is one of the largest organizations specifically focused on Black and Latino boys, especially within the context of education. Besides their conference, they have outstanding professional development and programming throughout the year. Check out their good work at www.coseboc.org or @coseboc.

Dr. Victor Rios

When I read *Punished: Policing the lives of Black and Latino Boys*, I was blown away by the clarity of insight by Dr. Rios. His sociological theory around the Youth Control Complex

---

[19] I loved how Peter Block included a section like this in his *Community: The Structure of Belonging*. I've borrowed the same format for this and the next book as well.

gave name to what I had been trying to explain for years and his work was a centerpiece of my doctoral work. When we met and shared a stage together in 2020 in Fresno, California, I appreciated the depth and humility of my Brother. Dr. Rios' work can be followed at https://drvictorrios.com/ or @drvictorrios.

■ ■ ■

Dr. Howard Stevenson

Dr. Stevenson is a quiet powerhouse in my world of supporting boys of color. His work in *Playing with Anger: Teaching Coping Skills to African American Boys Through Athletics and Culture* as well as his explanation of racial literacy have been very impactful in my thinking and practice. I was first introduced to this brilliant scholar through my colleague and close brother, Dr. Duane Thomas, both at the University of Pennsylvania at the time. Since then, Dr. Stevenson and I have had a chance to connect while he visited his home state of Delaware. Oh, and his younger brother, Bryan Stevenson, is pretty dope as well. Check out Dr. Stevenson's Ted Talk "How to resolve racially stressful situations."

■ ■ ■

Holistic Life Foundation

Born in Baltimore, this amazing organization is committed to nurturing the wellness of children and adults through yoga, mindfulness, and self-healing practices. I've come to know and continue to be inspired by two of the founders, my brothers Ali and Atman Smith. They have given access to healing and trauma-informed practices to many boys of color by keeping it rooted in their culture. From their work in Baltimore to their work with indigenous youth in Akwesasne, you've got to check them out at https://holisticlifefoundation.org/ or @holisticlifefoundation.

Living Justice Press

With the deepest commitment to help produce works that contribute to the best thinking around restorative practices, justice, and healing, I have admired the folks at Living Justice Press for some time. Getting to work with them on *Colorizing Restorative Justice: Voicing Our Realities* offered me the opportunity to be in community with some amazing authors and get access to outstanding books. Check out their great work at https://livingjusticepress.org/.

■ ■ ■

Amplify RJ: Restorative Justice Podcast

I got turned on to the work of David Ryan Barcega Castro-Harris a few years ago as a guest on his Amplify RJ podcast. I was moved by his clarity of purpose and thoughtful practice in just one conversation. I've been following his great work in calling the village of restorative folks together to share scholarship, application, and challenges within the work. Follow this progressive young voice at https://www.amplifyrj.com/ or @amplify.rj.

■ ■ ■

International Institute for Restorative Practices

The IIRP is the largest organization of scholarship and professional development in restorative practices in the world. Not only has it been instrumental in my initial training in RP but has continued to support my development and contribution to the evolution of the field. It remains a central place for practitioners across the spectrum to find each other to learn, share ideas, challenges and victories. Check them out at www.iirp.edu.

■ ■ ■

National Association of Community Restorative Justice

The NACRJ biannual conference has been a powerful site for grassroots, progressive and indigenous practitioners for over a decade. With heroes like Dr. Fania Davis and leaders like Dr. Teiahsha Bankhead and Lee Rush, the NACRJ has been a critical voice in both remembering the roots of restorative justice and advancing the field. I encourage you to get involved in their great work at https://www.nacrj.org/.

ROC Restorative

I've had the privilege of working with real practitioners in Rochester, NY for almost 10 years. Under Ms. Ruth Turner's committed leadership, the ROC Restorative team is one of the best examples of district implementation and community impact that I have ever experienced. Not just interested in school-based services, they have created the Restorative H.U.B. (Healing, Understanding, Belonging) as an intentional space for building community, navigating conflict, and restoring relationships. Learn more about their fantastic work at https://www.rcsdk12.org/domain/12268.

Transforming Lives Inc

It is something uniquely more challenging and special to do this good work with the most misunderstood and marginalized youth in schools. Transforming Lives Inc (Tli) was formed in 2017 to do just that. Each of the practices in this book are implemented in various forms across the schools and programs at Tli with youth placed in alternative education. I'm biased, but so very proud of the work that we do and the organization that we have built. You definitely want to see our work at www.tliservices.org.

Bibliography

* Abu-Jamal, M., & Lamont Hill, M. (2011). The Classroom and the Cell: Conversations on Black Life in America. Third World Press.
* ACLU. (2000). Affirmative Action - ACLU Position Paper. American Civil Liberties Union.
* ACLU. (2014). Why Single-Sex Public Education is a Civil Rights Issue. American Civil Liberties Union.
* Akoto, K. A. (1992). Nationbuilding: Theory & Practice in Afrikan Centered Education. Talkingstick Publishing.
* American Psychological Association. (2008). APA Zero Tolerance Task Force report. Retrieved from https://www.apa.org/pubs/reports/zero-tolerance
* Anglin, D., Alberti, P., Link, B., & Phelan, J. (2008). Racial differences in beliefs about the effectiveness and necessity of mental health treatment. American Journal of Community Psychology, 17-24.
* Ani, M. (1994). Let the Circle Be Unbroken: The Implications of African Spirituality in the Diaspora. Red Sea Press.
* ASCD. (2013, May). Why our schools are segregated. Retrieved from www.ascd.org: http://www.ascd.org/publications/educational-leadership/may13/vol70/num08/Why-Our-Schools-Are-Segregated.aspx
* Baldwin, J. (1992). The Fire Next Time. Vintage.
* Balkin, J. M. (2002). Is there a slippery slope from single-sex education to single-race education? Journal of Blacks in Higher Education.
* Baruti, M. K. (2015). Asafo: A Warrior's Guide to Manhood. Akoben House.
* Bomer, R., Dworin, J., & Semingson, P. (2022). Miseducating Teachers about the Poor: A Critical Analysis of Ruby Payne's Claims about Poverty. Teachers College Record.
* Bourdieu, P. (1984). Distinction: A social critique of the judgement of taste. Harvard University Press.
* Boyden, J. &. (2005). Children's risk, resilience, and coping in extreme situations. In M. Ungar, Handbook for working with children and youth: Pathways to resilience across cultures and contexts (pp. 3-26). Thousand Oaks, CA: Sage.

* Boyes-Watson, C. (2008). Peacemaking Circles and Urban Youth: Bringing Justice Home. Living Justice Press.
* Braithwaite, J. (1989). Crime, Shame and Reintegration. Cambridge: Cambridge University Press.
* Cabral, R., & Smith, T. (2011). Racial/ethnic matching of clients and therapists in mental health services: a meta-analytic review of preferences, perceptions, and outcomes. Journal of Counseling Psychology, 537-554.
* Chavis, B. (2009). Crazy Like a Fox: One Principal's Triumph in the Inner City. NAL Hardcover.
* Coates, T.-N. (2015). Between the World and Me. New York: Random House.
* Cooley, S., & Robertson, N. (2020). "Walk to Wellbeing" in Community Mental Health: Urban and Green Space Walks Provide Transferable Biopsychosocial Benefits. Ecopsychology.
* Courtenay, W. (2000). Constructions of masculinity and their influence on men's well-being: A theory of gender and health. Social Science & Medicine, 1385-1401.
* Davis, L. (1998). Working With African American Males: A Guide to Practice. Sage Publications.
* Dubois, W. (1903). The Souls of Black Folks: essays and sketches. Chicago: AG McClurg.
* Foster, D. (1991). 'Race' and Racism in South African Psychology. South African Journey of Psychology, 203-210.
* Franklin, A. (1999). Invisibility Syndrome and Racial Identity Development in Psychotherapy and Counseling African American Men. The Counseling Pschologist, 761-793.
* Gaylord-Harden, N., Burrow, A., & Cunningham, J. (2012). A cultural asset framework for investigating successful adaptation to stress in African American youth. Child Development Perspectives, 264-271.
* Gewertz, C. (2007, June 20). Black Boys Educational Plight Spurs Single-Gender Schools. Education Week, 26(42), p. 24.
* Gorski, P. (2008). Peddling Poverty for Profit: Elements of Oppression in Ruby Payne's Framework. Equity & Excellence in Education, 130-148.
* Gregory, A., Skiba, R. J., & Noguera, P. A. (2010). The Achievement Gap and the Discipline Gap. Educational Researcher, 39(1).
* Harper, N., & Dobud, W. (2021). Outdoor therapies: An introduction to practices, possibilities, and critical perspectives. Routledge/Taylor & Francis Group.
* Hattie, J. (2008). Visible learning: A synthesis of over 800 meta-analyses relating to achievement. International Review of Education, 219-221.
* hooks, b. (1995). Feminist Transformation. Transition: An International Review, 66, 93-98.
* Hubbard, L., & Datnow, A. (2005). Do single-sex schools improve the education of low-income and minority students? Anthropology and

Education Quarterly, 36(2), 115-131.
* Isaacs, M., Huang, L., Hernandez, M., & Echo-Hawk, H. (2005). The Road to Evidence: The Intersection of Evidence-Based Practices and Cultural Competence in Children's Mental Health.
* James, M. (2010). Never Quit: The complexities of promoting social and academic excellence at a single-gender school for urban African American males. Journal of African American Males in Education, 1(3).
* Jensen, E. (2013). How Poverty Affects Classroom Engagement. Educational Leadership, 70(8), 24-30.
* Kivlighan, D. M., Drinane, J., Tao, K., Owen, J., & Ming Liu, W. (2019). The detrimental effect of fragile groups: Examining the role of cultural comfort for group therapy members of color. Journal of Counseling Psychology, 763-770.
* Kosfeld, M., Heinrichs, M., Zak, P., Fischbacher, U., & Fehr, E. (2005). Oxytocin increases trust in humans. Nature, 673-676.
* Kunjufu, J. (2010). Reducing the Black male dropout rate. Chicago Heights: African American Images.
* Ladson-Billings, G. (1995). Toward a Theory of Culturally Relevant Pedagogy. American Educational Research Journa, 465-491.
* Lareau, A. (1989). Family-School Relationships: A View from the Classroom. Educational Policy, 245-259.
* Lareau, A., & Horvat, E. (1999). Moments of social inclusion and exclusion: Race, class and cultural capital in family-school relationships. Sociology of Education, 37-53.
* Lee Jr., J. M., & Ransom, T. (2011). The Educational Experience of Young Men of Color: A review of research, pathways and progress. Washington, DC: College Board - Advocacy & Policy Center.
* Lee, J. M. (2010). The Educational Experience of Young Men of Color. The College Board. Retrieved from https://secure-media.collegeboard.org/digitalServices/pdf/advocacy/nosca/nosca-educational-experience-young-men-color-research.pdf.
* Leuner, B., & Shors, T. (2013). Stress, anxiety, and dendritic spines: what are the connections? Neuroscience, 108-119.
* Lewis, S. (2009). Improving School Climate: Findings from Schools Implementing Restorative Practices. Bethlehem: International Institute for Restorative Practices.
* Lynn, M., Bacon, J. N., Totten, T. L., Bridges, T. L., & Jennings, M. E. (2010). Examining Teachers' Beliefs about African American Male Students in a Low-Performing High School in an African American School District. Teachers College Record, 112(1), 289-330.
* Martinez, E., & Davis, A. (1994). Coalition Building Among People of Color. Inscriptions(7), 42-53.
* McDougal, S. (2009). "break It down": One of the cultural and stylist instructional preferences of black males. The Journal of Negro Education, 78(4), 432-440.

* McGrady, P., & Reynolds, J. (2012). Racial Mismatch in the Classroom: Beyond Black-white Differences. Sociology of Education. Retrieved from https://doi.org/10.1177/0038040712444857
* McGrath, K., & Sinclair, M. (2013). More male primary-school teachers? Social benefits for boys and girls. Gender and Education.
* Mehan, H. (1996). Constitutive Processes of Race and Exclusion. Anthropology & Education Quarterly, 27(2), 270-278.
* Mitchell, A., & Stewart, J. (2013). The Efficacy of All-Male Academies: Insights from Critical Race Theory (CRT). Sex Roles, 69, 382-392.
* Myrie, Z., & Schwab, M. (2023). Recovery Experiences from Childhood Sexual Abuse among Black Men: Historical/Sociocultural Interrelationships. Journal of Child Sexual Abuse, 22-39.
* NASSPE. (2013). National Association for Single Sex Public Education. Retrieved from National Association for Single Sex Public Education: http://www.singlesexschools.org/schools-schools.htm
* NCES. (2009). Status and trends in the education of racial and ethnic minorities. National Center for Educational Statistics. Washington D.C.: U.S. Department of Education.
* Noguera, P. (2012).
* Payne, Y. (2011). Site of Resilience: A Reconceptualization of Resiliency and Resilience in Street-Life Oriented Black Men. Journal of Black Psychology, 37.
* Payne, Y. A., Starks, B. C., & Gibson, L. R. (2009). Contextualizing black boys' use of a street identity in high school. New Dir Youth Development, 123, 35-51.
* Pickett, L. (2020). Three Trains Running: The Intersectionality of Race-Based Trauma, African American Youth, and Race-Based Interventions. The Urban Review, 562-602.
* Riordan, C. (2002). What do we know about the effects of single-sex schools in the private sector?: Implications for public schools. In A. D. Hubbard, Gender in Policy and Practice: Perspectives on single-sex and coeducational schooling (pp. 10-30). New York: Routledge.
* Rios, V. (2011). Punished: policing the lives of Black and Latino boys. New York: New York University Press.
* Salomone, R. (2006). Single-Sex Programs: Resolving the Research Conundrum. Teachers College Record, 108(4), 778-802.
* Shaw, G. (2007). Restorative practices in Australian schools: Changing relationships, changing culture. Conflict Resolution Quarterly.
* Silveus, S., Schmit, M., Oliveira, J., & Hughes, L. (2023). Meta-analysis of culturally adapted cognitive behavioral therapy for anxiety and depression. Journal of Counseling & Development, 129-142.
* Speilhagen, F. (2011). It all depends...Middle school teachers evaluate single-sex classes. Research in Middle Level Education, 34(7), 1-12.
* Stanton-Salazar, R., & Dornbusch, S. (1995). Social Capital and the Reproduction of Inequality: Information Networks among Mexican-Origin High School Students. Sociology of Education, 116-135.

* Taft, C., & Creech, S. M. (2017). Anger and aggression in PTSD. Current Opinion in Psychology, 67-71.
* Task Force on the Education of Maryland's African American Males. (2006). Annual report of the task force on the education of Maryland's African American males. College Park: The University of Maryland.
* Thomas, D. E., Coard, S. I., Stevenson, H. C., Bentley, K., & Zamel, P. (2009). Racial and Emotional Factors Predicting Teachers' Perceptions of Classroom Behavioral Maladjustment for Urban African American Male Youth. Psychology in the Schools, 46(2), 184-196.
* Thompson, M., & Kindlon, D. (1999). Enabling Cain: Teach Boys Emotional Literacy or Else. Independence School, 88-92.
* Wald, J., & Losen, D. (2003). Defining and redirecting a school-to-prison pipeline. New Dir Youth Dev, 99, 9-15.
* Ward, E., Witlshire, J., Detry, M., & Brown, R. (2013). African American men and women's attitude toward mental illness, perceptions of stigma, and preferred coping behaviors. Nursing Research, 185-194.
* Whaley, A., & Davis, K. (2007). Cultural competence and evidence-based practice in mental health services: A complementary perspective. American Psychologist, 563-574.
* Whitehead, T. (1997). Urban Low-Income African American Men, HIV/AIDS, and Gender Identity. Medical Anthropology Quarterly, 411-447.

Acknowledgements

Medaase (I thank you in Ashanti Twi):

Once again, to my beloved, best friend, thought partner, and wife, Dr. Christina Watlington. Your brilliance and wisdom are shared throughout this book because you are so influential in my worldview and practice.

To Sadiki for being my fuel, fire, and example for what healthy manhood can become. I see you son and am honored to carry the spear and shield alongside you in this struggle for the liberation of a People.

To Ngozi for always allowing me to lean on your wise mind and get sharpened by the iron of our resident wordsmith. I'm looking forward to seeing that look and smile you make when you read something dope.

To my editor and friend, Malene Kai Bell, for such thoughtful feedback and support in getting this one done. You made this work so much better and helped me see what could be done with the project.

To the closest brothers in my Tribe of amazing men: Duane, Steve K., Darin, Steve B., Raymand, Will, Jon, Geoffrey, and Warren. You have held me up, gave me a good 'chin-check' when needed, and prayed for me always. Thank you for sharpening my saw.

To those ancestors, both personal and otherwise, whose spirit finds home within me: Rachelann, Lonnie Cochise,

Bobby, Arnold Stone, Lemuel, Malcolm X, Kwame Ture, and many more.

To our Akoben LLC and Transforming Lives Inc. tribes for your hard work and amazing commitment to serve our boys of color and all students. I sing the praise songs of you warriors everywhere I go.

Finally, once again, to those whom I didn't name, please blame it on my head and not my heart. Here is your chance to be acknowledged:

Thank you _____ for your _____.

(print your name here) (name your contribution)

About the Author

For nearly three decades, Dr. Abdul-Malik Muhammad has been serving both youth and adults as an educator, transformational leader, entrepreneur, and author. Always working with the underserved in urban and rural areas, he has focused on the development of boys to men, been active in social justice, and building progressive organizations. He has been a teacher, principal, career college president, corporate director of education, and vice-president of a national mental healthcare organization. Throughout this time, he has launched 25 schools and specialized programs, led a staff of 2,400 across 11 states and spoke on leadership and community building in 5 continents. He is currently the founder and CEO of Akoben LLC, a professional development company, and Transforming Lives Inc., a provider of alternative education services. Through this work, he is continuing to diligently "transform lives, one community at a time." He is the author of *The Restorative Journey – Book One: The Theory and Application of Restorative Practices* and contributing author of the recently released *Colorizing Restorative Justice: Voicing Our Realities*. He has a BA in International Affairs from Franklin & Marshall College, an MA in Educational Leadership from the College of Notre Dame of Maryland, and an Ed.D in Educational Leadership from the University of Delaware. He is a proud father of two grown people and lives in Delaware with his wife, Christina, and their 2 dogs.